BARRON'S

Katharina Schlegl-Kofler

Dalmatians

Photographs: Monika Wegler
Illustrations: Renate Holzner
Consulting Editor: Dan Rice, D.V.M.

CONTENTS

TYPICAL DALMATIAN

- Friendly
- Adaptable
- Very active
- Untiring
- Sensitive
- Happy
- Dependent
- Playful
- Aristocratic

The Dalmatian's athletic, elegant appearance, interesting markings, and winning personality make it one of the most popular breeds. Dalmatians are excellent family dogs; easy to train, they are very active dogs that love to run. Together with proper care and an appropriate diet, they need attention and regular exercise to be content. If you provide those needs, you'll have a vital, happy companion for many years.

MAKING UP YOUR MIND

1 Do all family members agree about getting a dog?

2 Is anyone in the family allergic to dog hair?

3 Are you prepared to devote most of your free time to your dog for the next 10 to 15 years?

4 Can you assure the Dalmatian won't be left alone for extended periods of time?

5 Are you aware that a dog is another family member and its training requires a great deal of time, persistence, patience, and consistency?

6 Are you willing to spend outdoor time with your pet in all types of weather?

7 Do you have an athletic and active lifestyle?

8 Have you calculated the cost of veterinary services, food, pet insurance, grooming equipment, collars, leashes, and other necessary items?

9 Can you tolerate white hairs sticking to the furniture, car seats, clothing, carpet, and elsewhere? Do you have ample spare time for grooming?

10 If you rent, are pets allowed in your home?

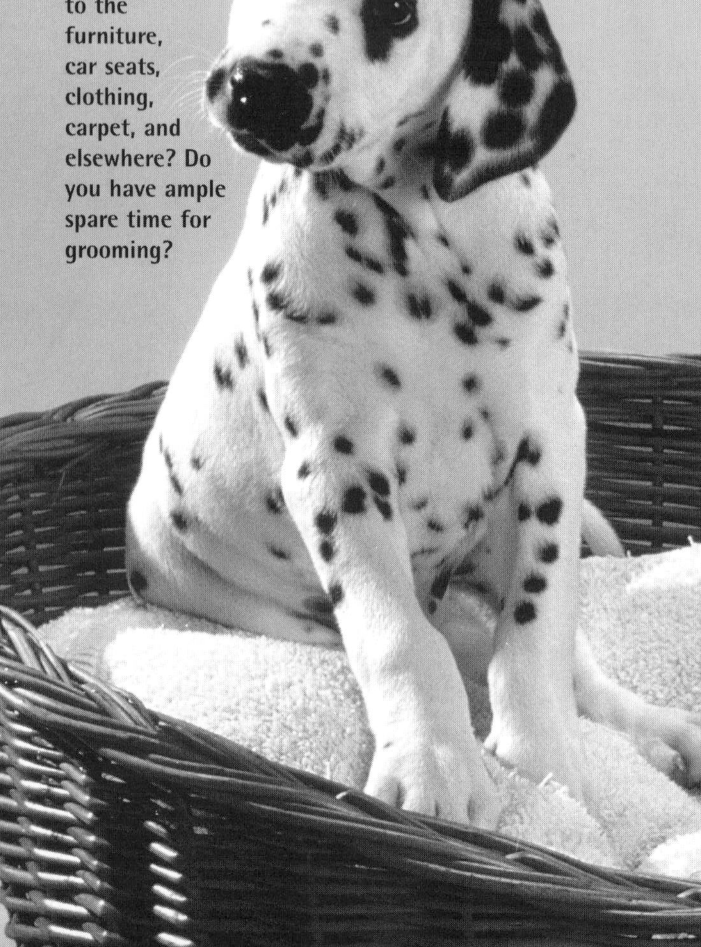

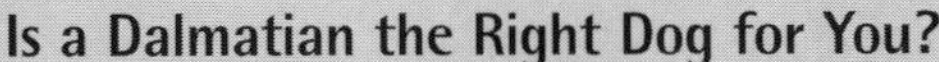

Is a Dalmatian the Right Dog for You?

You should consider a Dalmatian only if you have answered "Yes" to each of the foregoing questions. If you have decided to acquire a Dalmatian, you should be aware of the following:

✔ The purchase must be carefully planned.

✔ As with every dog, Dalmatians require basic and consistent training (see page 46) from puppyhood.

✔ Dalmatians make fine family dogs and generally adapt quickly to children (see page 29) and to other house pets (see page 28).

✔ Most Dalmatians are tireless playmates.

✔ Dalmatians need to be kept busy; they are active and get into mischief when bored.

PURCHASE AND ADJUSTMENT

Originally highly esteemed in Europe, this dog is becoming more popular and wins more friends every year. If you plan ahead, you and your Dalmatian should have many happy years together.

Origins of the Breed

Much of the Dalmatian's history is lost in antiquity, and has become obscured beyond explanation. Mutation, or genetic changes, probably account for the breed's unusual, small black spots on a pure white background. Selective breeding may have perpetuated this characteristic appearance. The origin of this beautiful dog goes back to the Egyptian period; a similar-appearing dog decorates the memorial slab at the grave of a Pharaoh dating from 2000 B.C. Paintings record comparable dogs in successive eras, and travel accounts mention them in a wide variety of places. In the paintings, these dogs are often pictured in hunting scenes and as companions on coaches, which is possibly why they are often called coach dogs. The designation "Dalmatian" first appeared in Thomas Bewick's *History of Quadrupeds*, published in 1771.

How Dalmatians Got Here

It is believed Dalmatians originated in the country called Dalmatia on the Adriatic coast and were transported to other countries by seamen. They were highly esteemed as companions on the coaches of the nobility, not only as guard dogs, but also for their distinguished appearance. In America these colorful dogs quickly became preferred companions for horse-drawn fire equipment. The loud barking of the Dalmatian cleared the way for the firefighters, and many contemporary fire departments keep Dalmatian mascots today, hence the nickname "firehouse dog."

At the end of the nineteenth century, Dalmatians enjoyed great popularity in England, and breeding them became a common endeavor. Wars and the worldwide replacement of coaches by automobiles took their toll on the breed, and the population of Dalmatians suffered severe setbacks. Because of the efforts of committed English Dalmatian lovers, however, the breed survived and continues to enjoy great popularity in many countries. Disney's Dalmatians in the movie *101 Dalmatians* caused sales to skyrocket and then plummet as owners realized that movie dogs and family dogs are different animals. Real dogs need to be trained, and that takes time, effort, and money.

Playful Dalmatian puppies love exploring in small caves like this one.

Where to Find a Dalmatian

As a Dalmatian owner you should check your dog's pedigree, even if it is to be a companion and you have no plans for Conformation showing, Obedience trials, or other competitive activities. Perhaps your best assurance of obtaining a typical, healthy Dalmatian (see page 4) is to buy a dog from a breeder of purebred Dalmatians who belongs to a breed club recognized by the American Kennel Club or Canadian Kennel Club.

Purebred Dog Associations: The Dalmatian Club of America (DCA) is the parent organization that oversees 30 or more regional clubs boasting more than 1,000 members. The DCA conducts an annual National Specialty Show and publishes a quarterly magazine entitled *The Spotter.* Further information about becoming a member of the DCA can be obtained by directly contacting the Dalmatian Club of America or the American Kennel Club (AKC) (see Information on page 62).

There are many sources for purebred dogs. Professional breeders advertise in national magazines; pet shops are also a source. Often, conscientious breeders post ads in veterinarians' offices and in newspaper classified ads. Veterinarians, neighbors, and dog fanciers may be able to provide advice on choosing a breeder and a puppy. The pedigree of a purebred puppy contains the designation "AKC" after the name, or initials of the breeder's regional association. A good way to get acquainted with other Dalmatian fanciers and their dogs is to visit a local, regional, or national specialty or all-breed dog show.

Note: You can discover locations and dates for dog shows by consulting the AKC or individual Dalmatian clubs.

The Right Breeder

To find the best breeder, you should visit several who are actively raising Dalmatians. An important factor to consider is the way in which the puppies are raised. Choose a breeder whose entire family handles the puppies, one who raises them in the home with the family and keeps the puppies and their surroundings clean. Puppy environment should be arranged to allow the pups to regularly come into contact with people, toys, and chewing items. The pups should not be isolated in a kennel. Puppies exposed to humans from very early in life learn to trust people. These pups approach visitors without fear, and generally are happy and emotionally steady. Beware of timid, shy, or fearful Dalmatian puppies.

Good breeders:

✔ Raise all their dogs in close contact with family members.

✔ Give the new owner a feeding schedule as well as some food for the first few days.

✔ Avoid raising several litters at once and have sufficient time to devote to the puppies.

Breeders to Avoid

A puppy mill offers several breeds for sale at the same time, and usually sells puppies it doesn't raise. Such an establishment is a poor place to obtain a good Dalmatian. Try to avoid dogs with a history of being housed in kennels or department stores. Never buy a sick puppy; don't allow pity to govern your selection. Above all, don't support dog traders or contribute to reckless exploitation of breeding females.

Puppy or Adult Dog?

Puppies usually require more attention than adult Dalmatians. Conversely, a puppy hasn't formed its personality and habits, and with proper knowledge, you can influence its best development (see Important Note, page 63).

With adults your control will be diminished and your authority will be reduced. Depending on the dog's previous experiences, you can expect some surprises, a few not pleasant. To minimize these events, you should discover as much as possible about the adult Dalmatian's past history.

Male or Female?

Male and female Dalmatians are equally devoted and affectionate.

Young Dalmatians test their strength by playing tug-o-war.

TIP

Standard Traits

Dalmatians are strong, muscular, lively dogs with great endurance. Their physique is well balanced and trim; their movements are powerful and rhythmical, with long, striding gaits. Dalmatian feet are round and firm, like cats' paws. They have a pleasant, friendly nature with no nervous, timid, or aggressive tendencies. A Dal's coat is short and smooth. The ground color is pure white; spots are either black or liver-colored, but never both colors on a single dog. In dogs with black spots, the eyes are dark; with brown spots, they are medium brown to amber. For females, the ideal size is between 21¼ and 23¼ inches (54–59 cm) at the shoulder; for males, between 22 and 24 inches (56–61 cm) at the shoulder, and about 60 pounds (27 kg).

Males generally need a firm hand in training and have a tendency to fight with other males. They are stronger and larger than females.

Females come into heat for about three weeks twice a year at intervals of six or more months. The owner must be attentive to this fact to avoid unwanted reproduction.

Choosing the Right Puppy

To assure a harmonious life together, it's important to match the dog to the owner. A person who is softhearted and nonassertive will probably *not* enjoy a domineering Dalmatian male. If you visit the litter often, you will observe differences in the puppies' personalities.

PORTRAITS: DALMATIANS

Two colors are acceptable in Dalmatians: spotted black on white, and spotted liver on white.

The proper distribution of the spots, called *spotting*, is also important.

Seven-week-old puppy with dark ears.

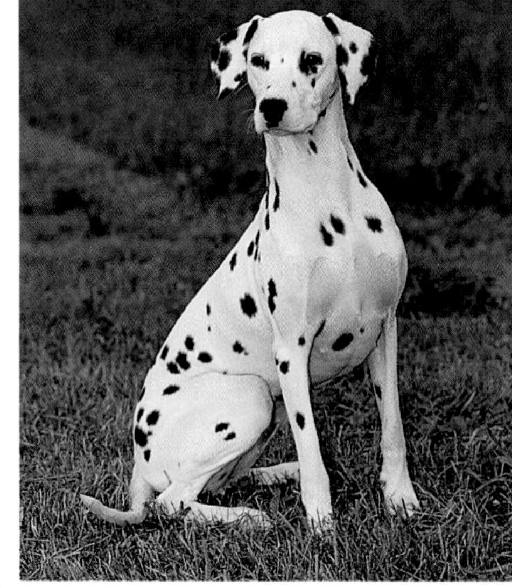

Above: One-year-old female with light to medium spotting.

Above: Two- and three-year-old females, strongly spotted with light speckling and nearly solid-colored ears.

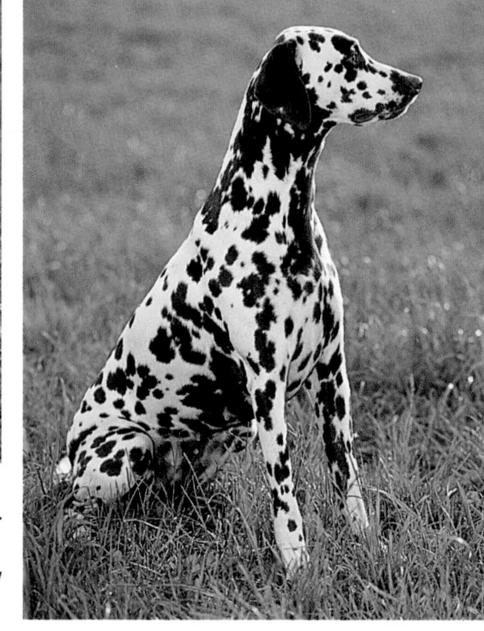

Right: Three-year-old female, strongly spotted and patchy, with speckling and dark ears.

Above: Three-year-old male, nearly optimal conformation, neat medium spotting, with marbled ears.

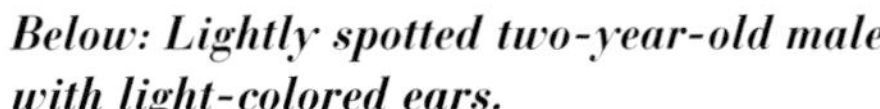

Below: Lightly spotted two-year-old male with light-colored ears.

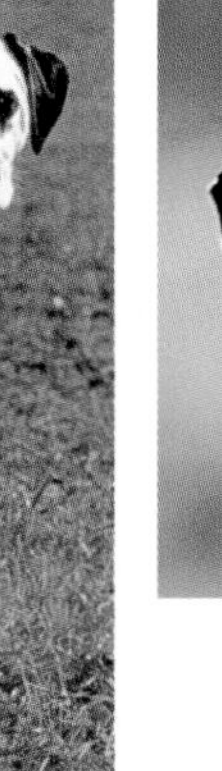

Above: Medium spotted female with nearly solid-colored ears.

Left: Seven-year-old female Dalmatian.

Right: The spotting isn't quite "finished" in puppies.

TIP

What to Look for

Canine coats that are genetically white often are associated with hereditary deafness. Dalmatians are subject to deafness, and brood stock should be tested for normal hearing before they are bred. Although no standard testing requirement prevails among breeders, some clubs offer evaluation of a puppy's hearing with a special test. Breeders can usually determine bilateral (both ear) deafness, but an audio test is required to test for unilateral (one ear) deafness. Ask about hearing when you buy a pup. Observe both parents to be sure they are free of skin disease, and are of normal disposition and temperament. They should behave normally, without timidity, nervousness, shyness, fearfulness, or aggressiveness.

If frequent visits are impossible, the breeder should be able to help you choose the type of puppy you will appreciate—the one that will match you best.

In general, puppies that jump up on people and bite their clothing are self-assured and aggressive. They don't like to be placed on their backs or dominated in other ways. A dominant pup will usually run ahead of you on walks, in contrast to a quiet puppy that exhibits friendly behavior such as licking your hand or offering a paw instead of jumping up. It lies relaxed on its back without resistance, and stays closer to you when you go for walks. This pup is better socialized, with a quiet personality.

The best time to make your final choice is when the puppies are about seven weeks old. You should try to take the puppy home no later than the tenth week.

Dog Shows

If you attend a local, regional, or national Dalmatian show, or an all-breed show, you may decide to show your dog. If that is your intent, you should purchase your puppy from a winning breeder (see The Right Breeder, page 10), who should be able to predict which puppy is likely to become a successful show dog. Occasionally, a companion dog, bought without regard to show potential, matures into a hand-

some Dalmatian and causes the owner to consider showing. Breeders are always pleased when a Dalmatian owner decides to show one of their outstanding puppies. AKC registration is a prerequisite for entering your Dalmatian in AKC-sanctioned shows.

What Do Judges Look for?

A dog show, considered by some a beauty contest, is held for the purpose of evaluating breeding stock. Physique, color, ring behavior, gait, and overall appearance (see TIP: Standard Traits, page 11) are judged. In addition, proper handling and presentation affects placement of your dog.

In all-breed shows, dogs are divided and shown according to group. Dalmatians are in the AKC non-sporting group.

Classes: Dogs are entered in classes according to their age, past show experience, and titles.

✔ Puppy—for dogs six months old, but under twelve months.

✔ Twelve to eighteen months

✔ Novice—for dogs six months and older, without three first place wins.

✔ Bred-by-exhibitor—for dogs bred and shown by the owner or a member of his or her family.

✔ American-bred—for dogs bred and whelped in the United States.

✔ Open—for any dog older than six months.

✔ Winners—for undefeated dogs of the same sex, having won first prizes in their earlier classes.

✔ Best of Breed—for champions of record and winners of the Winners Class.

At specialty shows held by Dalmatian clubs and at all-breed shows, the best Dalmatians vie for the coveted Best of Breed title.

Group: In all-breed shows, the winner of the breed class advances to the group competition. Here the Dal is up against all the other best of breed winners in the non-sporting group. The Dal's competitors include American Eskimo Dog, Bichon Frise, Boston Terrier, Bulldog, Chinese Shar-Pei, Chow Chow, Finnish Spitz, French Bulldog, Keeshond, Lhasa Apso, Poodle, Schipperke, Shiba Inu, Tibetan Spaniel, and Tibetan Terrier. The group winner will be the dog the judge considers the best representative of its breed.

Note: Registration forms and information are available in AKC publications or from the AKC (see Information, page 62).

Pet stores have a broad selection of toys for dogs of all ages.

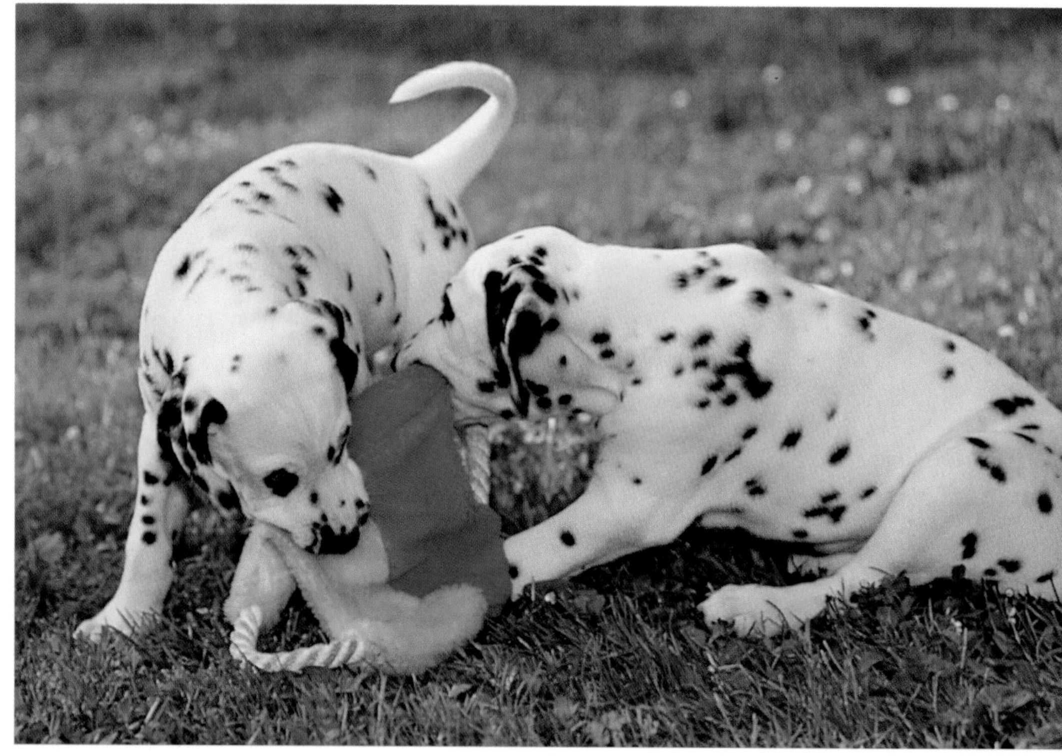

These seven-week-old puppies are enthusiastic chewers.

The Right Equipment

You'll need some basic equipment for proper care of your Dalmatian. To be ready for your puppy, you should shop for the equipment you need before bringing your Dal home (see Checklist, page 17).

Bed

The puppy's bed should be of appropriate size and located in a quiet, draft-free place. The best location is in close proximity to the family's activities. It should provide a retreat or den where the pup feels safe and secure, not in the way of the family, but near it. It should be washable and big enough to accommodate an adult dog, fully stretched out on its side (see illustration, page 19). Pet shops offer a broad selection of beds, baskets, and cushions.

Dog basket: A basket for an adult dog should be about 32 inches (80 cm) long. Baskets are suitable only after the Dal has finished teething (see page 37); otherwise, the wicker or other material will invite chewing by the pup.

Food and Water Dishes

Stainless steel dishes are rugged, stable, easily cleaned, and dishwasher safe. To avoid spilling the food, dishes should be large enough to accommodate an adult Dalmatian's meals without being filled to the brim. If your dog is an energetic eater, buy a dish equipped with a weighted base to hold it in place.

Collar, Lead, and Whistle

A leather or nylon web buckle collar is best for Dalmatians to wear every day. It must be adjustable for length. Chain or nylon training collars are commonly used for instruction.

Leashes made of leather, nylon, or chain are usually needed in several lengths for training exercises and walks.

Dominant or aggressive dogs that constantly pull against their collars and attempt to reach other dogs may require training collars or head halters for better control. Consult an experienced trainer for advice on the use of this equipment.

Whistles can be more effective than your voice at greater distances. Teaching a dog to obey a whistle requires consistency and extensive training, and you must carry the whistle with you at all times.

Toys

Dalmatians of all ages thrive on play. Various toys are available in pet supply stores (see illustration, pages 14 and 15). Purchase only safe dog toys such as hard balls, canvas retrieving dummies, and large, knotted ropes, and be sure to buy the correct size. Never give your dog soft rubber balls or other toys that can be chewed or have parts that can be swallowed. This includes squeaky toys.

Checklist Equipment

1. **A washable Dal-size dog bed.**
2. **Food and water dishes of appropriate sizes that are easy to clean, with weighted bases to hold them in place on the floor.**
3. **The correct amount of the food that the pup is used to.**
4. **An adjustable leather or nylon web collar, and an appropriate leash of similar material.**
5. **Dog whistle (not the silent variety) such as might be used for training hunting dogs. These are available from pet supply stores.**
6. **Several toys, constructed of safe materials and large enough that they can't be chewed up or swallowed.**

HOW-TO: WELCOME HOME

Being separated from its usual surroundings and its dam and littermates is a traumatic experience for any puppy. It is important to take every opportunity to make this adjustment as comfortable as possible for the pup.

The Smell of Home

A day or two before you pick up your puppy, give the breeder a towel to put with your puppy and its littermates; then when you take the puppy home, take the towel as well. Allow the pup to lie on it on the ride home, and put it in the pup's new bed. The towel will convey the familiar odors of the puppy's dam and littermates to its new home.

The Trip Home

Take a friend with you when you pick up your puppy. Your spouse or a responsible child will be recognized as a member of the puppy's new family, and it will be more at ease. If you are picking up the pup by public conveyance, ask about interstate travel regulations before the trip. Take along a collar, leash, and roll of paper towels for cleaning up any accidents. Buy a travel crate that has adequate ventilation and visibility; place the pup's towel inside the crate, and put it on the backseat. Talk to the pup in soothing tones, and pet it frequently. Play soft music on the car radio.

Note: The little Dalmatian should have nothing to eat for two hours before a car trip. If driving for a long distance, make a stop every hour to allow the pup to get out and move around. Be sure to keep the pup on a leash when outside the car!

Your new puppy will feel secure on an adult passenger's lap, but for safety's sake, put your little Dal in a crate with its blanket for the car ride home.

Arriving at Home

When you get home, immediately take the puppy to an area in your yard for bowel and bladder emptying. Let the pup explore its new home and get to know its new family slowly and calmly. Don't allow friends and neighbors to approach it right away. After a few days, invite friends and relatives to visit one at a time, but ask them to curb their enthusiasm. Let the puppy take its time making contact with visitors.

The puppy should always have its own feeding place with its own food and water dishes.

Perhaps the pup has already adopted a favorite toy; maybe it wants to nap. Show it a couple of toys and its sleeping place. After a few hours, give the pup its first meal in its new home.

House-training

The more attention you give your puppy, the more quickly it will be house-trained. Take your Dal to its spot in the yard immediately after each nap, after meals, and in the middle of play periods. Return it to that area any time it sniffs the floor intently or begins to turn in circles. Always take it to the same spot in the yard. As the puppy becomes acquainted with this and makes the connection between the area and the odors of previous eliminations, it will begin to understand what it has to do. Praise the pup each time it eliminates outside.

Limit the puppy's freedom at night by placing it in a large box or portable pen. When it needs to urinate or defecate, it will let you know by its restlessness. It's not natural for a pup to dirty its sleeping place. When you hear your Dal moving around, carry it outside, wait until it performs, then praise it and return it to its box.

If you observe the puppy defecating or urinating in the house, simply pick it up and carry it immediately to its backyard spot. Don't scold or reprimand the pup in any way; it is performing a perfectly natural act. Thoroughly clean the area of its elimination using a nonammonia-type disinfectant. It is important to rid the spot of the scent of eliminations to prevent your Dal from using the spot again.

The right way to carry a puppy: One hand supports the rear end while the other supports the back.

The Sleeping Place

Puppies are accustomed to sleeping with their littermates. That was their pack, and the security and nearness of the pack comforted the pup. For that reason, it's best to put the pup's bed close to its new pack's sleeping site. Place the bed near your bedroom, where you can hear its restlessness, indicating a need to relieve itself during the night.

The puppy should not be disturbed while it is sleeping.

DAILY CARE AND MAINTENANCE

When treated fairly, Dalmatians are adaptable, uncomplicated family members. To prevent any problems from beginning, it is important to know as much as possible about your puppy's development and its proper care.

What Dalmatians Are Like

Dalmatians are facinating dogs that require a great deal of exercise and close family bonding to be content. They don't adjust well to confined or sedentary living, and are much happier in active, outgoing families. They are sensitive dogs that thrive in well-adjusted, friendly families where they can assume an active role. If kept in good condition and well nourished, Dalmatians are happy, lively, and playful. They make excellent companion dogs and partners for various dog sports such as Agility and Obedience (see pages 50–51). They enjoy a game of hide-and-seek or fetch and are excellent partners for joggers, horseback riders, and, under properly controlled conditions, they enjoy running beside bikes (see photo, page 20). Dalmatians have natural hunting instincts similar to those of many other breeds. This natural behavior becomes a problem if they are allowed to run free and unsupervised. A typical Dalmatian is temperamental, but not nervous, and adjusts well to children as well as other house pets (see page 28). As with any dog breeds, Dals need basic, consistent training from the time they are young (see pages 24 and 48–49).

The Dalmatian should always run on the right of the bicycle, and only on bikepaths and rural roads that have little traffic.

The Puppy's Development

The first 20 weeks of a puppy's life are the most impressionable. Influences, experiences, and training that occur during this period are imprinted on the dog's mind, and won't be forgotten; therefore, fill this period of your Dalmatian's life with positive acts and experiences.

Birth to eight weeks: This early period is the canine socialization time when puppies are introduced to littermates and, sometimes, other dogs. Human socialization also begins during this time, when the pup views early human contacts the same way as canine contacts. Human relationships and experiences the pup has at this young age provide the foundation for trusting people. Interesting surroundings and the opportunity to interact with its environment can have a very positive effect on the puppy's development. This points out the need to select a conscientious breeder from whom to buy your Dalmatian (see page 10)!

Eight to about fourteen weeks: This period is an impressionable phase of a puppy's life when it finds itself included in a new environment with various humans. Learning social skills, deportment rules, and limitations is of primary importance. Nest etiquette is forsaken in favor of human regulations. This is the time in which the Dal's role is defined in its new family, and consistent training should begin immediately. The pup must learn its name and simple commands, and must become accustomed to wearing a collar. Petting, feeding, and praise for correct performance are positive reinforcements that should accompany this training. A Dal should not be overprotected, but must become accustomed to its total environment. New noises, different terrain, stairs, traffic sounds, and an endless variety of people will become part of its new life. It must be introduced to other dogs under your supervision, and learn proper canine behavior. For this, the best possible exposure comes through puppy kindergarten or play sessions with dogs its own age (see page 23).

The second six months of life: During this time your Dalmatian will reach sexual maturity and may exhibit occasional disobedience or lack of focus. You must consistently remind it of the social rules in force. Your persistence and consistency will reinforce the trusting bond between you and the pup and will gain respect from your Dalmatian. You will be established as the highest-ranking partner or alpha pack member (see page 24).

Sexual maturity: This is obvious in the female when she comes into heat (see page 29). Maturity in a male is indicated by leg-lifting when urinating.

Adult Dalmatians

At about two years, all traces of puppyhood are left behind. If you have taken your Dal's training seriously, you now face many years of pleasant companionship. You and your family will be the center of your dog's life.

Dalmatians may live 12 to 15 years. You can tell when senility is approaching by the effort the dog takes to get up in the morning. Your Dal will exercise with less enthusiasm, and it may become more

Puppies can be taught to climb stairs by playing games.

The Dalmatian's Development in the First Year

First Year (impressionable stage)	*First and Second Weeks of Life* Puppy is nearly helpless; searches for milk and warmth are already important experiences. *Three to Eight Weeks* Puppy is increasingly mobile and interested in exploring its surroundings. It is more susceptible to the influence of humans and other dogs. *Nine to About Fifteen Weeks* The puppy takes its place in human society. Strong bonding develops with its home, owner, and new family. *Fourth and Fifth Months* The young dog becomes more independent and willful. It avoids rules and tests the alpha leader of its pack.
Six-month-old Dalmatian	The most impressionable stage is finished. If successful training and bonding have taken place, you are the center of focus of your Dalmatian and are accepted as the alpha or highest ranking partner.
Second Year of Life	The Dalmatian is sexually mature: Females are seasonally cycling; males begin marking. Puberty is sometimes accompanied by another stage of independent, willful behavior.

sensitive to foods. The TIP on page 58 discusses some special ways to treat an aging dog.

Puppy Playtime and Training

Structured playtime courses contribute to the development of your Dalmatian and teach it proper canine behavior.

Puppy playtime: From the age of about nine to sixteen weeks, your pup should attend puppy kindergarten where groups of six to eight puppies of similar ages and sizes are put together to learn to behave properly with other dogs. Their self-confidence is promoted through play, collective experiences, and visual and auditory impressions. At the same time, the owner picks up valuable information and learns how to give commands that are easily accepted by the puppy. The most important aspect of these sessions is play, not training. Puppy kindergarten is usually sponsored by dog clubs, but may be offered by private agencies or a group of individual dog owners.

Training courses: The older Dalmatian puppy is of moderately long attention span. By six months, its concentration is sufficient to join a Canine Good Citizen course in which dogs and their owners work in small groups under the supervision of a trainer. Before beginning the first session, learn the rules of conduct. You can order the rules from the AKC (see Information, page 62).

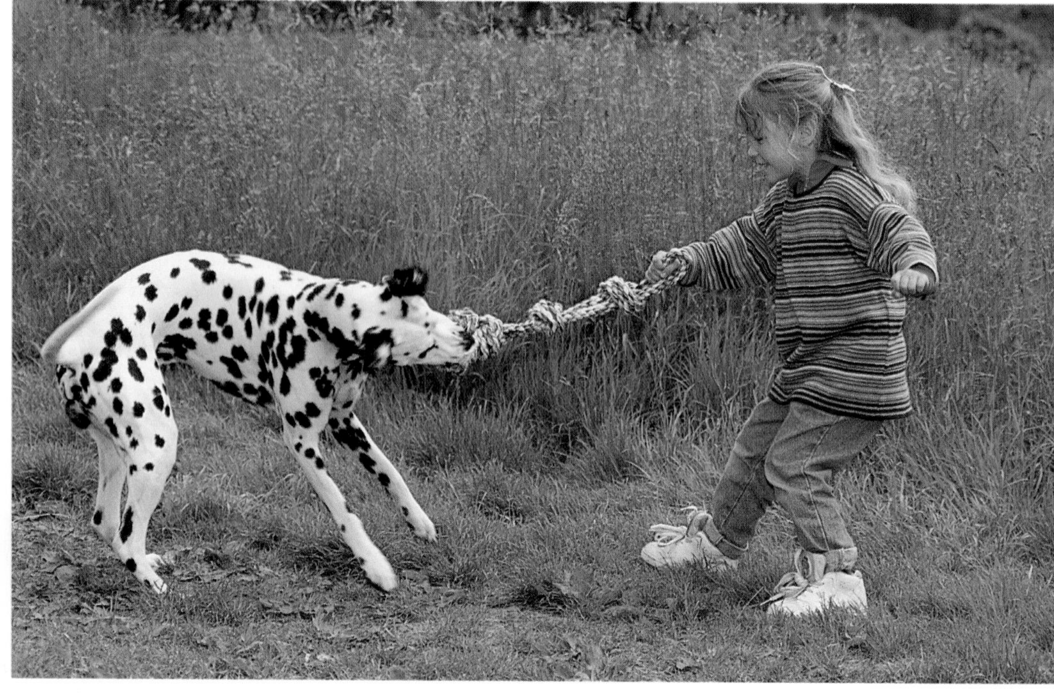

Both are winners in a game of tug-o-war.

Dominance Training

In order to survive, the pack takes direction from the chief, or alpha, dog, an instinct that surfaces in house dogs as well. If you follow certain guidelines, your Dalmatian will have no problem accepting you as the superior partner; it won't be concerned with survival and you will provide your puppy security and trust.

The following points are basic.

✔ The dog must focus on you, not the other way around.

✔ You must be consistent and persistent in all training. Insist on observance of the rules and prohibitions you have established.

✔ Don't allow the dog to jump up on the sofa, chairs, or bed. These elevated comfort areas are reserved for higher-ranking pack members.

✔ Feed the dog after you eat. Lower-ranking pack members always eat after you and your family.

✔ Don't tolerate your dog's defense of its food, sleeping place, or toys. While it is still a puppy, take its dish away for a short time periodically while it is eating.

✔ Maintain authority over the dog's toys and chew bones. If the dog readily tolerates having its toys taken away, give them back after a few minutes. If it growls, withhold them and return them only when the dog exhibits friendly behavior.

✔ Roll the dog on its back at odd times. Flex its legs, play with its toes, and scratch its belly.

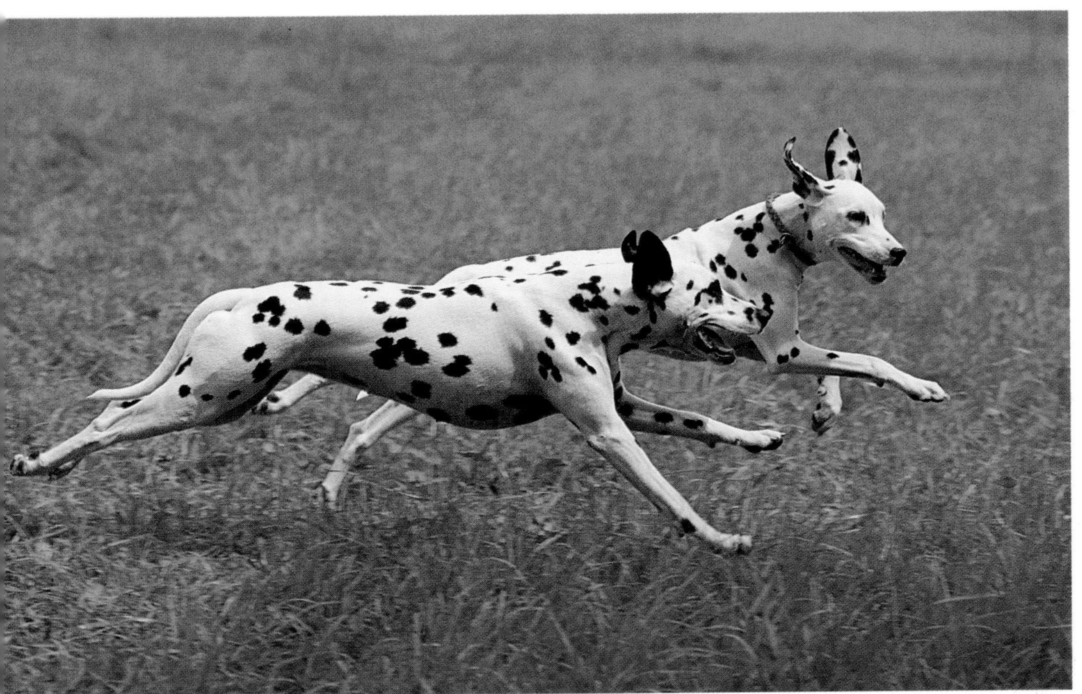

Romping is a good way for your Dal to expend excess energy.

These actions reinforce your alpha dominance and the dog's subordination to you.

Playing with a Dalmatian

Just as playing with other dogs is important, so is playing with the family. Frivolous activities that are fun for you and the dog promote bonding and teach valuable lessons about living together. Don't submit to the Dalmatian's agenda; always make the decision to play when *you* want to, and end the sessions when you wish.

Teach your dog not to bite. Begin when it's a puppy and never allow it to mouth your clothing or any part of your body. When you play tug-o-war, be sure the dog doesn't win every time. Make playtimes more interesting by putting toys out of reach when not being used. This will teach the dog that you will dictate when playtime begins and when it stops.

Daily Exercise

Puppies: Dalmatians are energetic dogs, but take care not to overexercise young puppies.

✔ Take the pup for several short walks rather than a single, long jaunt.

✔ Puppies that haven't completed their vaccination program should not leave your yard. Check on leash laws before you exercise your pup off lead.

✔ When you exercise older pups off lead, change directions occasionally or hide to teach

TIP

Legal Protection

For your peace of mind, and in order to avoid possible legal problems, here are some suggestions:

✔ As soon as possible, investigate insurance policies to protect you from liability in case your dog destroys someone else's property or bites someone.

✔ Dog-proof your car to assure that your Dalmatian is secure in it. If the dog rides in a cargo area of a van or station wagon, separate that area from the passengers' space by a grate or net. If your dog rides on a seat, provide it with a canine seat harness.

✔ Ask local authorities about regulations governing the use of leashes or muzzles, and be sure to register your dog and fasten its tag securely to its collar.

your Dal to concentrate on you and your whereabouts.

✔ If you call your dog with no response, run a short distance to encourage the puppy to follow you more closely.

✔ Playing with other puppies the same age and size will usually not be harmful unless the other dog has a contagious disease.

✔ As your Dalmatian ages, you can begin to take longer walks with it.

Grown dogs: At the age of one year, Dalmatians can take as much exercise as you can handle. Walks of an hour or two will suit the dog fine, and it will enjoy longer outings, weather permitting; your Dalmatian has a short coat and may prefer a warm house to a lengthy walk on a cold day.

Getting Accustomed to a Bicycle

Running beside a bicycle can be dangerous for the rider and the dog. Dogs on leashes may run in front of the bike, upsetting the bike and injuring you and the dog. Special considerations must be learned before attempting this form of exercise. Never take a dog into automobile traffic while you are riding a bicycle. Well-conditioned dogs may endure extended trips of 6 to 12 miles (10–20 km) when they are accustomed to biking.

✔ When your dog is trained, it will always stay on the right side of the bicycle.

✔ Biking with your dog requires special commands to teach the dog its proper position.

✔ To train the dog to accompany you on your bicycle, first push the bike while leading the dog. When the dog has learned what to expect, you can try to carefully mount and ride.

A special spring is available that can go on the bike frame, to which the lead is attached. This piece of equipment will help prevent accidents.

Riding in the Car

Many Dalmatians have no trouble riding in cars, while others don't tolerate automobile travel well and need assistance. The following tips can be useful:

✔ Gradually accustom the dog to riding by taking short, slow drives over straight roads.

✔ Associate the short drive with a pleasant experience, such as play, a walk, or some treat. The Dal will soon realize that a fun time follows a drive.

✔ If the dog is prone to car sickness, ask your veterinarian to prescribe a preventive medicine.

✔ Take a friend along on the first few trips. The driver can concentrate on the car, and the helper can watch the dog.

Very young dogs can be held on your lap (see illustration, page 18) or placed on the

10 Golden Rules
for Young Children

1 Dogs feel that they are equals with small children; therefore, young children should never correct the dog or try to take away its bone, dish, or toy, unless an adult is supervising.

2 Toddlers should not give commands to the dog.

3 Young children should not bother the dog while it is eating.

4 Children should not play vigorously with the dog.

5 Avoid games with the dog that place the dog in a dominant role.

6 Small children should avoid playing with the dog unless an adult is nearby.

7 When the pup is tired or bored, children should refrain from encouraging it to continue. Allow it to rest or sleep undisturbed.

8 Young children should be taught not to annoy or hurt the puppy.

9 Sick or injured puppies should be handled carefully—only by adults.

10 If a dog shows a desire to be left alone, the child must immediately respect the dog's growling and retreat.

floorboard. When your Dal is two months old, it can be placed in the cargo area of a van or station wagon, which has been separated from the passenger area by a grate or net. In other cars, fasten the dog into a special harness on the backseat.

Getting Acquainted with Other Animals

Horse: If you plan to have your dog accompany you on horseback rides (see photo, page 29), familiarize it with horses while it's young. Carry it into the stall of a horse that has been around dogs extensively. When the two animals have been introduced, put the pup on the ground and watch it and the horse closely until they are cautiously friendly.

House pets: Young animals adapt to one another more quickly than older ones. When introducing two pets to each other, keep the pup on a leash for the first few meetings to reduce the stress on the other pet. Don't bet on an adult Dalmatian becoming good friends with hamsters, guinea pigs, mice, or even birds that might be considered prey and trigger instinctive hunting behavior in your dog.

Meeting Other Dogs

Female dogs usually meet males without much trouble. Females meeting other females may do well if both dogs are spayed, or if neither is in heat. Males are usually more aggressive and often, when two males of similar sizes meet, a confrontation follows. If neither male is leashed, and owners don't interfere, both dogs may sniff a bit and go on their way. If one male is leashed and the other is not, however, there may be problems. The best plan is for the free-running dog to be leashed; then carefully allow the dogs to become acquainted through sniffing and play. Dogs should be trained very early to respect other dogs, whether on or off lead. If a scuffle or fight ensues, take care in breaking it up. Canine Good Citizen training will help to defuse these situations (see page 50).

✔ To avoid being bitten, never reach between the dogs in a fight. Usually, the confrontation will last only a few seconds, and one dog will then back off.

✔ Spraying the combatants with a garden hose will usually break up the fight.

✔ Always carry a squirt bottle full of water and use it if a fight starts.

With mutual respect, dogs and children will become fast friends.

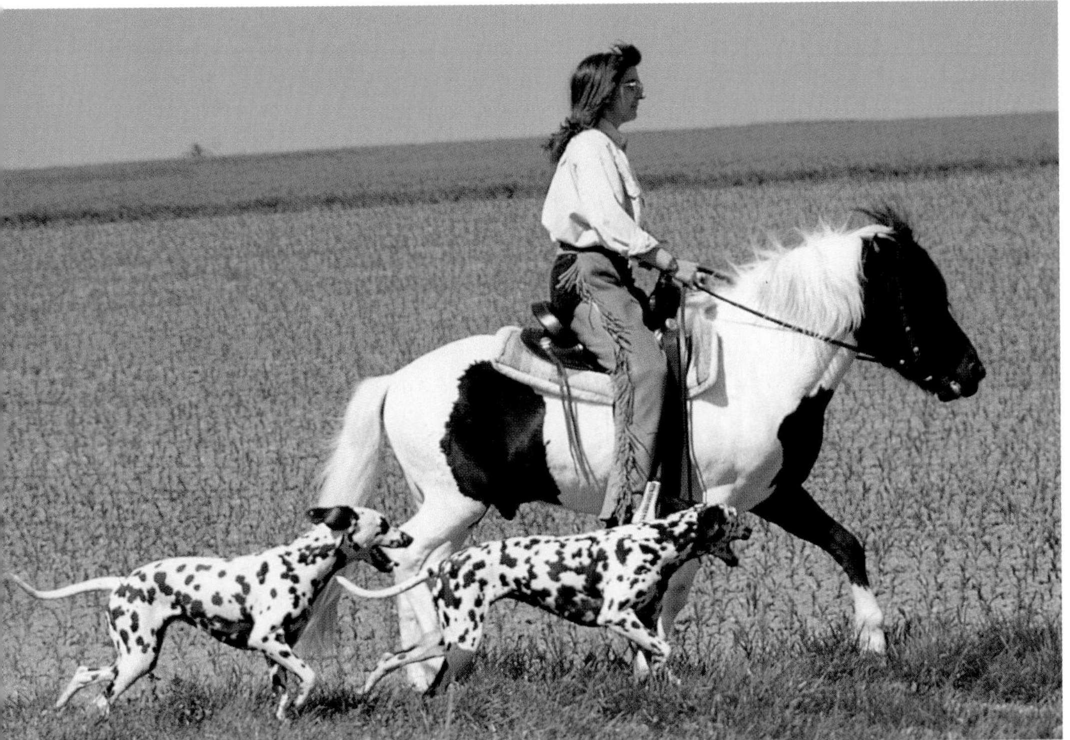

A well-trained Dalmatian is an ideal comrade for a ride in the country.

Keeping More than One Dog

If you're planning on acquiring a second dog, consider the following:

Start with one: Since a new pup will imitate the actions and habits of the older dog, it's best to wait until your Dalmatian is well trained and exhibits desirable behavior before introducing another pup.

Male and female: Dogs of the opposite sex usually are more compatible than same-sex pairs. Remember that females come into heat every six months or so. If you plan to add a new dog to your family, consider having females spayed and males neutered (see page 58).

Dogs of the same sex: Two males or two females in the same household will be more compatible if a significant age difference separates them. Neutering both dogs will also help prevent confrontations. To avoid conflicts, don't add a dog that will clearly be dominant to your existing pet.

Dalmatians and Children

Wait until your children are three or four years old before introducing a Dalmatian into the family. This serves two purposes: Children of that age require less concentrated care, so you will have more time for a pup, and four-year-olds are

VACATION WITH A DALMATIAN

Be sure all vaccinations are current.

Don't feed the Dalmatian anything for several hours before starting on the trip.

Pack the dog's luggage, and include food, dishes, brushes, blanket, toys, and your whistle. Don't forget the Dal's collar and leash.

If you plan to travel interstate or across national borders, check requirements in the state or country into which you will be traveling, as well as those of your home state or country.

Assemble a first aid kit for your dog. Include items to treat digestive disorders, injuries, and motion sickness. If you are planning to leave your dog in a boarding kennel, make necessary arrangements early.

capable of understanding how a pup should be treated. Dalmatians are robust, stable dogs that do well in family situations. They are hardy and tolerate children's handling, and they are affectionate and tireless playmates. Compatibility with children is an individual characteristic and depends on puppy experiences and circumstances encountered at the breeder's kennel. If the pup had positive experiences with children, it will probably continue to do so in your home, if it is treated with kindness and love.

Family dog training: If your puppy has had no contact with children, and is reserved with them, it should be introduced carefully to its new playmates. If the puppy is aggressive, it must be taught not to be rough with the children; the sharp teeth and toenails of a rowdy, aggressive puppy can inflict serious damage and instill fear and apprehension in children.

What children should be taught: The Dalmatian pup is not a stuffed toy. It is a living creature with its own needs, and should be respected. The important rules children should observe are listed in the Golden Rules on page 27.

Older children: Puppy care is fun and older children will enjoy being involved with the new dog and its care (see pages 36 and 37). Obedience training and early routine training can be shared with children over the age of 10 or 12, depending on their natural ability and interest.

Traveling with a Dal

Plan ahead. Ask about pets when you book reservations. Ask if dog restrictions apply to the beach or park you are planning to visit. Check on leash laws, dog-sitting services, and day care for your Dalmatian while you visit amusement parks or museums.

If you are traveling by car, take a break at least every two hours to exercise your Dal.

Keep it on a leash and exercise it only in designated places. Carry a jug of bottled water for the dog. *Never* leave your dog in a parked car; it's always hotter in the car than outside. Every summer dogs die needlessly because owners left them in the car "for just a few minutes."

If the Dalmatian Stays Home

Arrange for a pet sitter if you can't take your dog with you. Perhaps a neighbor who already knows the Dal will take care of it in your home. Some local breed clubs have members or telephone numbers of people who will take Dalmatians into their homes for a week or two. If necessary, reserve a spot in a good boarding kennel. Call in advance and, before booking, visit the facility and judge its cleanliness and its care staff.

Let animals get used to one another while they're young.

Pet Sitters

Word-of-mouth recommendations from your dog-owning friends are a good way to find a local reliable pet sitter. A professional sitter will include in his or her fee a preliminary visit to your home to get acquainted with your Dal, discuss details of your dog's care while you are gone, and present his or her credentials and references. Observe how your pet acts toward the sitter. If your Dal is not accepting of or comfortable with this visitor, look for another sitter.

The sitter should also provide you with:

- ✔ Literature describing services and fees as well as precautions to ensure the security of your home while you are gone
- ✔ A form for you to fill out that includes information about where you can be reached in an emergency, phone numbers of a neighbor and your veterinarian, details of medication, and other important data
- ✔ A service contract
- ✔ A service rating form for you to fill out upon your return

For more information, contact Pet Sitters International, a professional association of pet sitters that will put you in touch with members in your area (Information, page 62).

Proper Nutritition

Dogs are not true carnivores, even in the wild; their diet includes fruits and vegetables. For this reason, a strict meat diet doesn't serve their needs.

Prepared Dog Foods

Packaged dog food is reasonably priced and easy to store, prepare, and feed. High-quality diets should be fed without any supplementation or additions. They are balanced and complete with all the nutrition needed by healthy dogs. If they contain an American Association of Feed Control Officials (AAFCO) label, you can be further assured they are proven by actual feeding trials. Foods that have this label stating they are balanced for all stages of canine life are your best buy. Those labeled specifically for puppies, working dogs, pregnant bitches, giant breeds, or older dogs can be used if your Dal is in one of those categories. Don't make the mistake of feeding a balanced ration, then adding supplements to it.

Canned food: If balanced, this food may be fed exclusively or mixed with other balanced foods.

Dry food: This food may be complete and balanced as well. It may be fed by itself or mixed with canned complete and balanced food.

Complete diets: These are formulated for your puppy or adult that is not under stresses such as injury, pregnancy, heavy training, or work. Balanced and complete mean just that!

Soft, moist food: This packaged food appears to be meat, but isn't. It is more expensive than other foods, and contains preservatives that sometimes cause excessive water consumption. Its palatability and color seem to be the strongest selling points.

Canine Nutritional Needs

Few if any of us have the time, ability, knowledge, or facilities to prepare food that delivers all the nutritional needs of a dog. We would need a laboratory to analyze the vitamin and mineral content of each ingredient, as well as a colony of dogs to feed it to. Commercial dog food manufacturers routinely use feeding trials to test their formulas; however, there is a great deal of difference among brands. Check

It's important to feed a high-quality, complete, balanced diet.

Healthy puppies are playful, curious, and adventurous.

the labels and formulas of generic, commercial, and premium brands. If you want a healthy, vital, beautiful Dalmatian, leave its nutrition to the experts with years of experience, who have proved their diets on hundreds of thousands of dogs.

Supplements and Additives

Supplementing a complete and balanced diet is unnecessary. The addition of meat, eggs, or other foods only throws the dog's balanced diet out of balance. Oil or fat supplements fall into the same category; they are rarely necessary, and they upset nutritional balance. Vitamin-mineral supplements may be indicated in certain circumstances; they don't add protein, carbohydrates, or fat to the diet. Check with your veterinarian before you buy supplements that may be used to treat skin and coat disorders, or aid in the recovery from illnesses.

Chew Supplements

Dogs naturally chew. If you don't furnish your Dal puppy something to gnaw on, it will chew furniture, shoes, gloves, and anything else that fits in its mouth. Nylon bones provide hours of chewing and are not harmful. They will keep your puppy or adult dog out of mischief when you are away and will strengthen its jaws and help clean its teeth. Rawhide chew sticks are also great, but they usually don't last long. These short sticks formed from tiny pieces

Rules for Feeding

1. Food should be lukewarm, never served directly from the refrigerator or too hot.

2. If your dog doesn't eat its meal in a few minutes, discard the leftovers and offer less for the next meal.

3. Try to feed your Dalmatian at the same times each day.

4. Keep your dog quiet for an hour after each meal. This is a fundamental rule in order to help prevent gastric torsion or bloat (see page 56).

5. Don't add too much water to dry food.

6. When you find a food that is palatable and nutritional, stay with it. When changing diets, gradually mix the new with the old food in increasing amounts over a period of a week.

7. Don't feed table scraps or human food of any sort. This includes meat, cooked bones of any kind, and chocolate (or other candy). Also, avoid feeding cat food.

of untanned leather and molded together are favorites of active chewers. Reports of stomach problems associated with the larger twisted rawhide chew bones make them less attractive. Pig ear cartilage, cattle hooves, and cured tendons are other safe chew supplements. Never leave your Dalmatian alone without something to chew on.

Water Is Important

Canines can live for weeks without food, but they can't survive more than a few days without water. Your Dalmatian deserves the best. Offer it a fresh bowl of water no less than once a day, or more often if you are feeding a dry dog food. If the Dalmatian's water bowl is exposed to outside elements, refresh the water after a rain- or windstorm.

Note: Dogs need more liquids in their diets when stressed by illness or work, and on hot days.

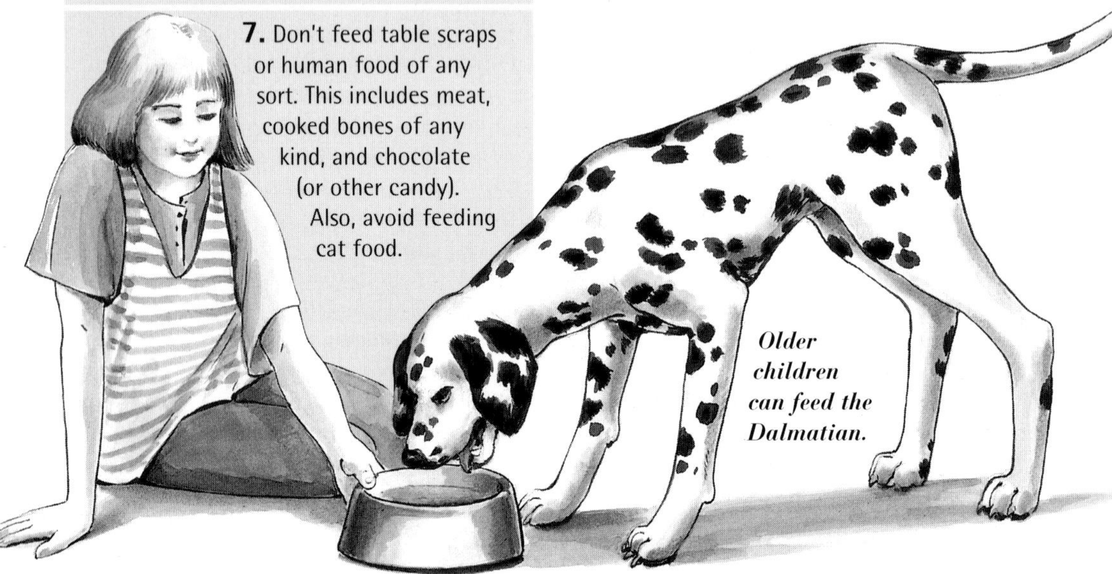

Older children can feed the Dalmatian.

Sample Feeding Plan for an 8- to 12-week-old Dalmatian Puppy	
around 8:00 A.M.	Complete and balanced canned puppy food or dry puppy food that has been dampened with hot water until about the consistency of hamburger or cottage cheese. Pick up and discard any leftovers in 10 minutes.
around noon	Repeat the 8:00 A.M. diet in slightly less quantity. If it is easier, you can feed canned food mixed with dry. If not eaten in 10 minutes, pick up and discard the leftovers and feed that much less at 4:00 P.M.
around 4:00 P.M.	Repeat the noon feeding quantity, using the same foods and technique.
around 8:00 P.M.	Repeat the early morning meal. The dog should be kept quiet at least half an hour before and one hour after this meal. At bedtime, give the dog a chew stick and a nylon bone to chew on.

How Much Food Does a Dal Need?

The daily quantity of food required depends on the dog's size, age, activities, and health status. In the beginning, use the recommended guidelines printed on the package. Weigh your adult dog once a week, and note if it is gaining, losing, or maintaining a desirable weight. In growing puppies, you should be able to feel the ribs beneath the skin, but they should not be visible. Dogs in training require more nutrients; working dogs have a higher demand as well.

✔ Ribs shouldn't stick out, but should be easily palpable with the flat of your hand.

✔ Puppies should maintain some soft fat beneath their skin.

✔ If you reward your dog with treats between meals, keep the treats minimal or use commercial treats that may be incorporated into its diet.

✔ Obese dogs aren't healthy pets. If your dog becomes overweight, ask your veterinarian to recommend a special diet.

How Many Meals a Day?

Puppies: Young, growing dogs require more calories per pound of body weight than adults; therefore, they should be fed more frequently, beginning with four meals a day for tiny pups, and gradually reducing the number until adulthood is reached.

The feeding chart on this page gives an example of a feeding plan for a puppy.

Adult dogs: Although some authorities feel that adult dogs can be fed once daily, you will find the dog is happier and healthier, with better eating habits, if fed twice daily.

HOW-TO: GROOMING

Proper grooming contributes to the Dalmatian's health and well-being. Regular care helps prevent illnesses and makes it possible to identify any early signs of illness that may occur (see page 55). The dog should become accustomed to your care and grooming while still a puppy.

✔ Always describe aloud what you're doing, such as "brush," or "eye check."

✔ When the Dalmatian is accustomed to your announcements, it will more easily accept examinations by the veterinarian and dog show judges.

Ear Care

Down or drop ears, such as those of Dalmatians, lack the ventilation of erect ears and, therefore, are susceptible to otitis, an inflammation of the ear. To care for Dal ears, moisten a cotton ball with alcohol and clean the outer ear canal. It should always appear clean, free from odors, and without inflammation or excessive wax deposits.

You should regularly clean your Dalmatian's ears.

Eye Care

Occasionally, a dog will have a slight secretion gathered in the nasal (inside) corner of the eye. This is seen more frequently in the early morning, and should be wiped clean with a dampened cotton ball. Healthy eyes are clear and free of redness.

Coat Care

Shorthaired Dalmatians need brushing to remove dead hair from their coats. Regular grooming will prevent much of their shed hair from being spread over your furniture and clothing. Brushing your Dalmatian daily or several times weekly will maintain a healthy coat.

Equipment: Use a bristle brush or rubber currycomb. A special glove with tiny rubber projections works quite well on the Dal's coat.

Brushing removes dirt and dead hairs, and massages the skin.

A coat care massage fosters your dog's sense of well-being.

✔ Regular grooming promotes healthy skin and coat and helps you bond with your pet.

✔ Most dogs enjoy the massage of a brush, rubber currycomb,

Feet and Legs

Pads: Check the footpads regularly. If dry and cracked, rub in a bit of Vitamin A&D ointment or lanolin. Wash the salt from the dog's feet after it has walked on salty roads or sidewalks. Beware of pad burns from running on hot summer pavement.

Claws: Toenails need to be checked regularly. They shouldn't touch the ground or click on the floor as the dog walks.

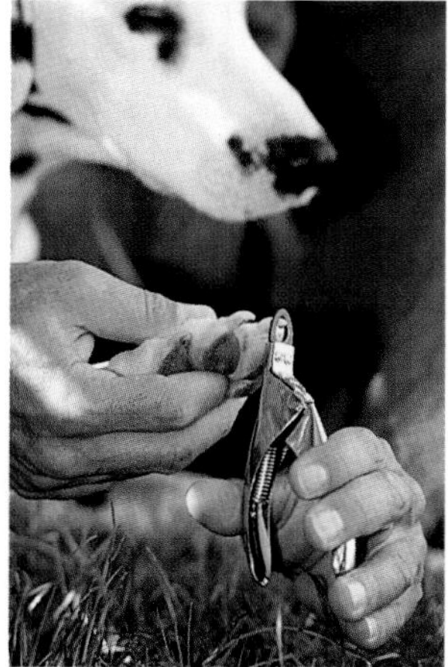

Careful! Don't damage blood vessels when you trim the claws.

If the dog runs on asphalt, nails don't usually need trimming. Puppies and old dogs' nails often need your attention.

Elbows: Calluses, caused by lying on hard surfaces, often need care. If inflamed, sore, or draining, have them examined by a veterinarian. If thick, dry, and cracked, treat them as cracked footpads with A&D ointment or lanolin.

Tooth Care

Proper feeding will help maintain a healthy mouth, as will regular tooth brushing.

Deciduous teeth: Baby, or deciduous, teeth begin to shed at about three or four months. Chewing habits are usually exaggerated at this time. Nylon bones or hard dog biscuits aid in normal tooth shedding. By six months, all deciduous teeth should be replaced with the adult set. If this is delayed, and double teeth exist, consult your veterinarian.

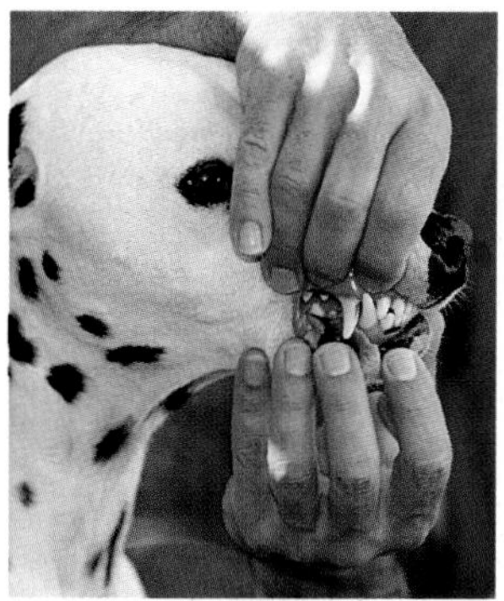

Checking the condition of the teeth.

chamois cloth, or grooming glove (see photo at left).

✔ A dog appreciates its owner's attention and the pleasant sensations that go along with grooming. This time of grooming and soft conversation is never wasted and will enhance the relationship between dog and owner.

Bathing

Swimming in clean water does no harm to the coat, but soap and water baths should be reserved for the times when they are definitely needed. Baths are indicated when your dog has rolled in mud or a pungent carcass, or when bathing will help in removing the dead hair of seasonal shedding.

✔ Use only dog shampoos that contain no insecticides unless skin parasites are the target of your effort.

✔ Dry the dog thoroughly with towels or warm-air hair dryers after bathing and keep it inside the house until completely dry.

Breeding

If you have an outstanding Dalmatian who has proven herself in the show ring, you may decide to breed her. Dalmatians commonly have large litters, and finding good homes for all of them is your responsibility. The only logical reason to breed any dog is *to improve the breed.*

✔ A tremendous amount of time and knowledge is required to properly breed dogs. You must be dedicated, and your motives must be pure, not self-centered.

✔ Space requirements inside and out are significant. Consider the number of puppies and the time it takes to place each one. While they are with you, they are *your* obligation and require *your* attention.

✔ There are many financial obligations. A litter of 12 Dal puppies all require vaccinations, food, and care.

Dogs Suitable for Breeding

Breeding-quality females are rare. Only females who have won their classes in Conformation shows are suitable to include in the Dalmatian gene pool. Temperament and disposition must also be considered. Dogs who show any tendency toward shyness, timidity, or aggressiveness should not be bred. Questionable marking, hereditary defects, and deformities must be considered. For instance, never begin a breeding program with a dog that has not been certified free of hearing difficulty as well as hip and elbow dysplasia. Pedigree examination and evaluation should be extensive in order to match a male with a suitable female. Talk with long-time reputable breeders. If you can honestly say your dog meets these standards, you may be ready to raise puppies.

A Dalmatian bitch will typically whelp 10 to 12 puppies, all of which will need good homes.

Fewer males than females are qualified to join the gene pool. Only rare, nearly perfect Dalmatian males are used for stud. They are typically the outstanding show winners who have proven their ability to reproduce fine Dalmatian characteristics.

The Biological Side

A good litter is not an accident; parents must be matched to encourage the production of favorable traits and discourage the propagation of faults in their offspring. Their pedigrees must be studied in order to find the best possible match. Offspring from previous litters of both the male and female are studied. Your local Dalmatian club can furnish the names of breeding advisors.

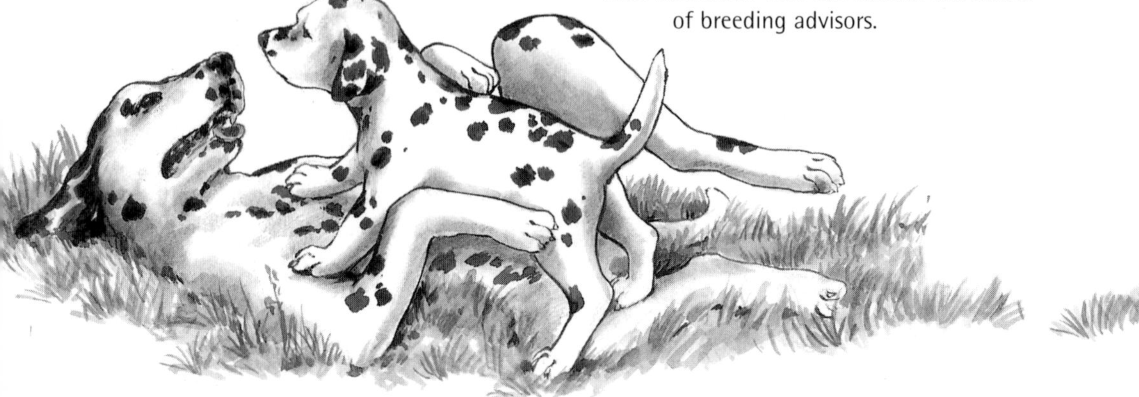

A female generally has two heat periods a year, each lasting about three weeks. Females will aggressively seek males during their estrus period, and must be kept away from them.

Mating: Bitches will conceive only if mated at the proper time. Generally, breeding couples are put together on approximately the ninth day of a female's heat. After breeding, they should be separated for a day, then bred again. Males have a gland on the shaft of their penis that is captured and held inside the female's vagina during copulation. This normal *tie* lasts about 20 minutes.

Pregnancy: Moderate exercise is important for a pregnant female. During early gestation, she will not require additional food and may be exercised normally. After about three weeks, her diet should gradually be increased and her exercise decreased. Some breeders feed puppy food during this time.

Birth: After a gestation of about 63 days, pure white Dalmatian puppies are born. If you observe any problems in the whelping, contact your veterinarian. Spots begin to appear on the pups over the first few weeks. Puppies consume only their dam's milk for three or four weeks, after which they can begin eating semisolid food. At that time, make available to them dry puppy kibble, well soaked with hot water.

TIP

Dalmatians: Fashion Dogs?

Dalmatians have become quite fashionable. They are beautiful, intelligent dogs that have been featured in movies and television in recent years. When a breed catches the public eye, it usually suffers from overexposure and indiscriminant breeding. Backyard breeders sprout up everywhere and the breed suffers. Greed promotes the mating of average dogs to substandard bitches—with disastrous results. Quality is forsaken in favor of numbers of puppies produced. If you have truly fallen in love with your Dalmatian companion, remember the standards you looked for and, if you can't improve the breed by mating your bitch, have her spayed. If you want another Dalmatian, go to a reputable breeder for a relative of your dog.

Raising a litter of puppies requires work and time.

BEHAVIOR AND ACTIVITIES

Dalmatians are active, eager learners that must be physically and mentally challenged. To promote appropriate habits, good health, and adaptation to your lifestyle, you should know about the characteristics of this breed.

Behavior is partly instinctive and partly learned. Before you can modify behavioral traits, you must communicate with your dog. Communication is a two-way street; you must understand your dog and your dog must understand you. This communication includes body language, voice, and physical and visual contact. Communication leads to understanding; understanding leads to compatibility.

Communication

Your dog will soon learn every phase of your communication. It will quickly recognize your voice and understand the various tones you use. Hand signals, touch, and even scent are picked up and remembered by the dog, never to be forgotten. It will recognize anger, pleasure, praise, and sympathy by your vocal tones.

Learning Dal Language

Pay close attention to your dog's body language to learn what it feels, what it understands, and what it is about to do. Raised hair on its neck or back, a stiff gait, and ear position are all messages to you, as are its tail carriage and interest in scent marking.

Threatening behavior: If your dog bares its front teeth and stares steadily at another dog, it is telling you that a confrontation is imminent. If it is uncertain of its position, or if it is frightened, your dog will draw the corners of its mouth back with parted lips. It will tuck its tail between its legs and will stretch its ears back close to the head.

Submissiveness: A dog wishing to greet a superior dog will hold out a paw, wag its tail, lick the dog's muzzle, and lie down to make itself very small. Puppies will often urinate while submitting to another dog. If an actual confrontation takes place, accompanied by snapping and biting, one dog may surrender. This is shown by the dog lying on its back exposing its tender stomach, with its tail tucked, its ears held tightly to the head, and its lips drawn back over clenched teeth.

Playful behavior: This body language takes the form of pushing with the muzzle and jumping and running in circles, and often includes lowering the forequarters to the ground and tossing the head to encourage the other dog to play.

Playing with human friends is an important aspect of bonding for the Dal.

Vocalizing

Growling: Dogs give warnings by growling. This sound means they recognize something suspicious, and they are about to defend themselves or threaten an antagonist.

Howling and whining: Pain is signified by howling in a pitiful way. Whining can represent anxiousness, boredom, excitement, uneasiness, or submissiveness.

Barking: Excessive barking is not a Dalmatian trait. Barking usually tells you the dog is excited or happy, but it might also be a warning, depending on the tone of the bark.

Communicating by Scent

Dogs have a well-developed sense of smell, a major means of communication. They sniff other dogs' droppings to discover who was recently in the area. Sniffing a dog's anal glands and facial scent glands is much like humans shaking hands. Urinary marking denotes a dog's territory, and a female's vaginal discharge may communicate her desire to find a mate.

Communicating by Touch

Touching each other by licking, nibbling, or lying close is an expression of friendliness and affection. In near confrontations, pushing or jostling another dog signifies dominance, as does the laying of its head over the back of another dog. Grasping the subordinate dog's muzzle in its mouth is still another means of communicating dominance.

How Your Dalmatian Understands You

Body language: Human body language tells our dogs what our intentions are. When you greet a puppy or strange dog, if you lower your body to its level, it will perceive no threat from you. If you stand tall and strike a defensive posture, the dog may back off, realizing your intent to defend yourself. Staring directly into a dog's eyes will cause it to become frightened. It may sink to submission or rise to challenge you, but since it can't understand the reason for your body language, it will be confused. It is your job to be sure your body language communicates your thoughts and intentions.

Voice: This is an important element in communication. Your tone, speaking speed, pitch, and volume give the dog as much information as the words you pronounce. Try to always use the same tone when you praise your Dalmatian.

Physical contact: By petting and cuddling your dog, you build trust and confidence. Gentle grooming accomplishes the same thing (see page 36). Dogs express their affection in other ways that humans might not appreciate, such as licking or jumping up.

Scent: Olfactory power, or the ability to determine scent, is far better developed in dogs than in humans. By interpreting pheromones or other scents, a dog often knows when a human is happy, frightened, excited, or otherwise stressed. This exceptional sense of smell accounts for a dog's ability to recognize us before we are seen or heard.

Combination of elements: Clear signals are necessary to let your dog see, hear, and understand your directions. Our voice modulation must match the words we speak. Praising a dog in a gruff voice is confusing to the dog. Deliberate use of communication elements is essential if the dog is to understand what we want and whether we are angry, playing a game, giving a command, or calling it to supper.

To avoid behavior problems, establish the ground rules of communication from the beginning. Be sure that all family members use the same commands. If you want your Dal to get off the sofa and tell it "Off!" and your spouse says "Down!" and your kids say "Geddown!" "Hey!" and "Excuuuuse me!" the poor dog will become confused. If it does not know what is expected of it, two things will happen: First, it will be impossible for you to properly train it. Second, it will develop behavior problems that are an extension of its confusion. These can include inappropriate elimination in the house, chewing, digging, barking, and aggressive behavior.

TIP

The Dalmatian Grin

Dalmatians often display a grin when they meet a person they like. This grin is expressed by curling the upper lip, showing the upper teeth. It is accompanied by laying its ears tightly against its head. The grin lasts only a moment and should not be confused with baring the teeth in a threat. It is a nonaggressive facial expression. The Dal also curls the upper lip when it invites you to play. Although the grin occurs in other breeds, it is characteristic of the Dalmatian. It is interesting that this behavior is displayed only toward people. Be sure to explain this to your friends who are meeting the dog for the first time, so they won't be alarmed.

Lowering the forequarters is a Dal's typical invitation to join in a game.

DALMATIAN BODY LANGUAGE

If you want to learn Dalmatian language, you must interpret your dog's behavior correctly.

My Dalmatian displays this behavior.

What is my Dalmatian trying to communicate?

This is the right way to react to this behavior.

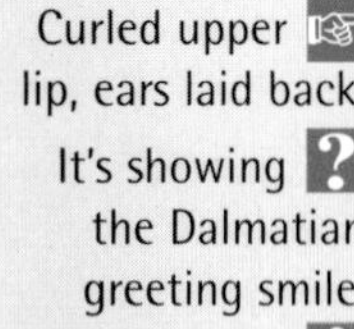

Curled upper lip, ears laid back.

It's showing the Dalmatian greeting smile.

Greet the dog in a friendly fashion.

Puppies crawl into a hollow log.

They're exploring their surroundings.

As long as there is no danger of injury, let them continue.

A male Dalmatian is marking.

He is leaving a message for other dogs.

Interfere only if he is supposed to be obeying a command.

Two Dalmatians are playing together.

Contact with other dogs is important training.

Let their playfulness continue.

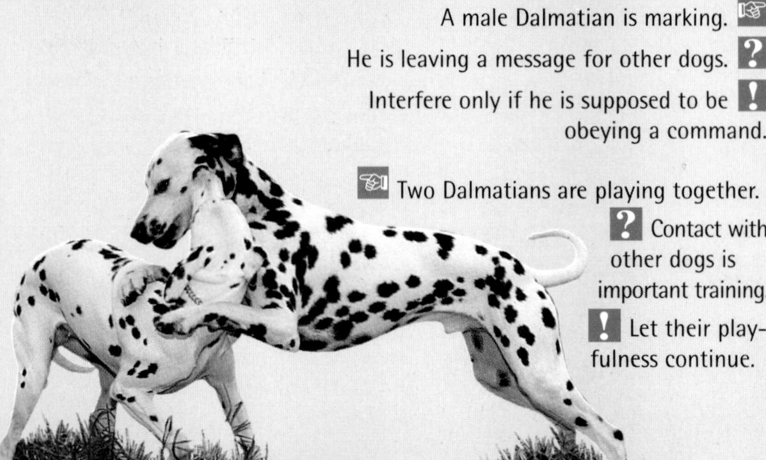

Confident Dalmatians meet one another.

? They're checking each other out.

! Don't interfere as long as they are acting friendly.

The Dalmatian is frozen in a pointing stance.

? Its body language tells of the scent of an animal.

! Call the dog to you.

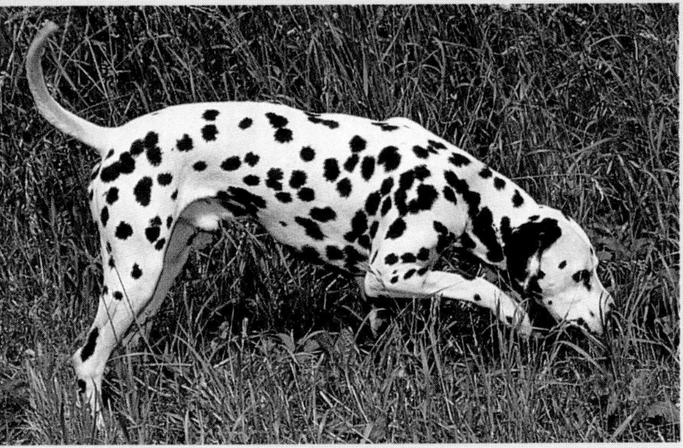

The Dalmatian is sniffing intently.

? Its nose has discovered a track scent.

! Call the dog to you.

The Dalamatian is barking.

? It's calling your attention to something.

! Investigate the reason for the barking.

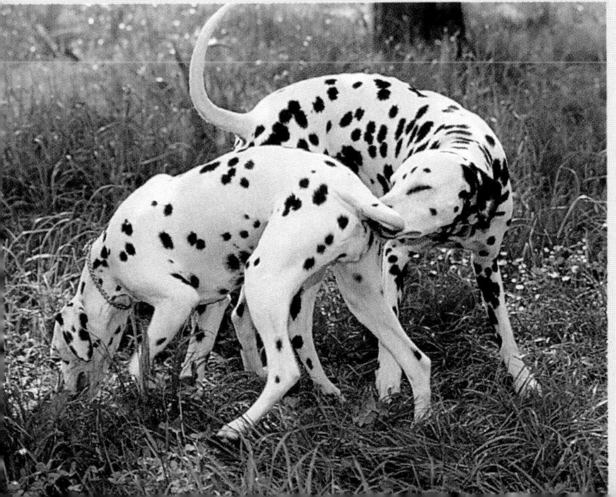

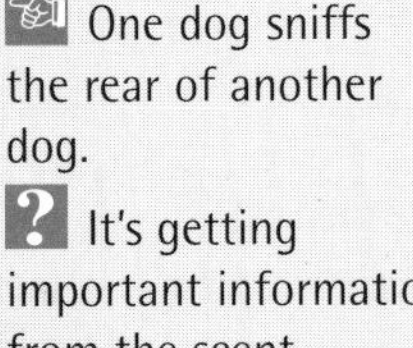

One dog sniffs the rear of another dog.

? It's getting important information from the scent.

! Don't interfere; no harm is being done.

HOW-TO: TRAINING

Every Dalmatian should be familiar with the following commands. Instruction sessions should take no more than five minutes per exercise and can be repeated two or three times daily. Give rewards only when the command is executed correctly. You may use food rewards, but you should always use generous praise and petting. After an exercise is learned, it should be repeated at least once a week to keep its performance fresh in mind.

Note: Always speak the dog's name in a normal voice before you give any command.

The treat held above the nose and moved toward it causes the puppy to sit.

Sit

Give the command "*Sit,*" and hold a treat above and in front of the dog's nose. Gradually move your hand back, over the dog's muzzle. The dog should sit without physical help, but if not, you can gently push the dog's rear to the ground. Reward performance with petting and a treat.

When it sits, it is given the treat.

The treat causes the puppy to take the down position correctly.

Down

This next command requires more effort. While your dog is sitting, give the command "*Down,*" offer a treat held directly under its chin, and gradually move it downward. The dog will usually drop to its chest. If it doesn't, gently push the dog's back down or take a foreleg in each hand and gently stretch its forelegs until its elbows are on the floor. Once it has performed, praise the dog and give it the treat. After a couple of seconds, release it with an excited "*O.K.,*" and move away.

Remember not to reward the dog for trying, only for performing correctly!

Heel

Early in training, the leash should be held in your right hand and run through your left to keep the dog at your left side and its muzzle even with your thigh. Say the dog's name, followed by the command "*Heel,*" then move forward slowly. As the dog moves with you, encourage it with soft speech. Don't snap the training collar. This exercise is not natural for dogs—be patient! Hold the dog back if it tries to move ahead, and encourage it forward if it lags. After a dozen paces, stop and tell the dog, "*Sit.*" When it sits, reward it with praise and a treat. Repeat the exercise several times, rewarding only correct performance. Then take off the leash and play with the dog for a few minutes. Heeling is boring and pointless to the dog and must be taught gradually.

Stay

This exercise always follows the *sit* or *down.* Using the appropriate command, put your dog in one of those positions. As you give the next command, "*Stay,*" place your open palm immediately in front of the dog's muzzle, then back away a few paces without speaking. After a few seconds, resume your place on the dog's right, give the dog praise and a treat, and release it from the exercise with a happy *"O.K."* This exercise is repeated only a few times the first day. Later, move farther away from the dog; it will learn to wait for your releasing command before it moves from the position in which you placed it. Eventually, you can teach it to release from the *stay* by calling it from across the room.

Come

When your puppy is very young, or your dog is new, each time you feed it, say its name and give the *come* command. This will teach the dog to pay attention when it hears its name, and it will learn that *commands mean rewards.* Each time you give the *come* command and your Dalmatian runs to you, give it generous praise on arrival. If you step into the yard or house, and you see your dog turn and begin to run to you, give the *come* command as well. When it arrives at your feet, crouch down and make a fuss over the dog. The dog will think it is always right, and it will always be ready to respond to you. Food rewards are fine when convenient, but the *come* command should always be rewarded with praise and petting. A whistle may be substituted for the *come* command, but that means you must always carry the whistle, which may be inconvenient.

Practicing the commands when feeding teaches the dog to come to you cheerfully and promptly.

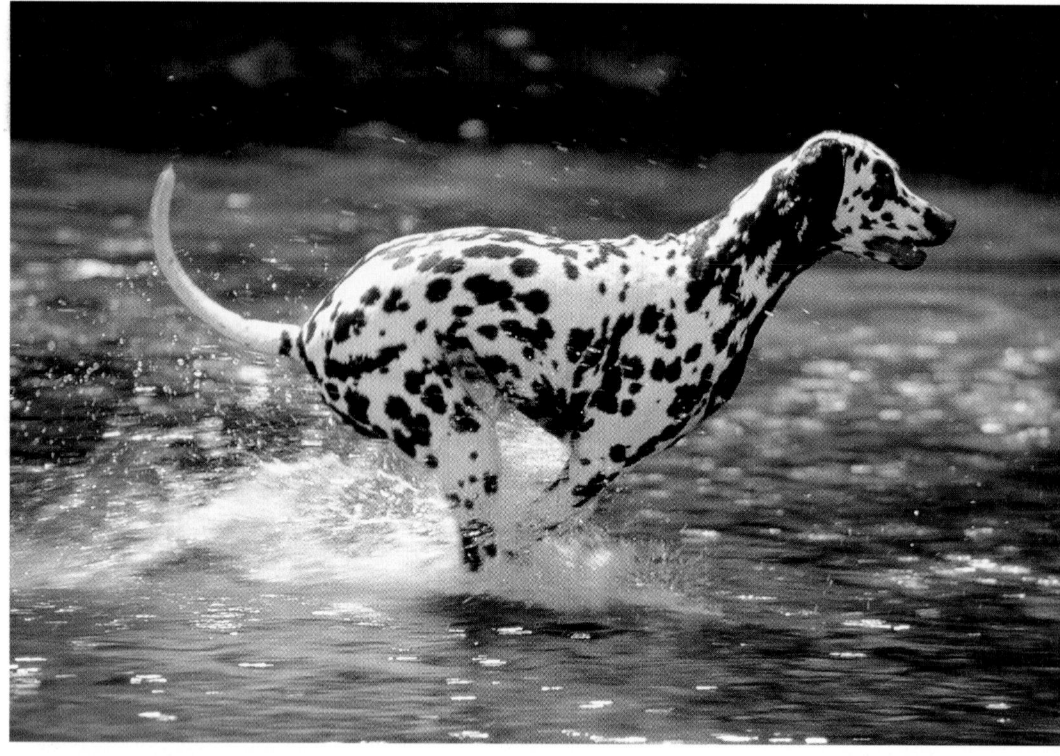

Many Dalmatians love swimming and romping in the water.

Training for a Happy Life Together

Keep your dog's focus on *you*, and make yourself as interesting as possible. Act excited and happy when your dog performs correctly. Don't forget you are the alpha dog in your household, and subordinates such as your Dal must respect and obey your commands. Never punish for disobedience; it's better to ignore a failed command and renew your training efforts. Never reward the dog for performing *almost right*. If needed, repeat the dog's dominance training (see page 24). Instead of immediately starting over on the failed command, revert to a simpler exercise that has been well learned and practice it before you try teaching the failed exercise.

Training: Training should be a shared effort between dog and owner. Don't delegate!

✔ To keep your dog motivated, don't spend more than five minutes per session on an exercise.

✔ Don't repeat commands. Always follow the same routine: Say the dog's name, hesitate, and issue the command.

✔ Begin and end each training session with an exercise the dog has mastered. Never allow training sessions to interfere with regular play sessions.

Preventing problems: From puppyhood on, humans must take a superior role to the dog in all cases.

✔ Regularly reinforce dominance training. Take the dog's food away while it is eating; move your dog from its favorite resting place and take that place for yourself. Insist on respect at all times and never tolerate challenges to your alpha dog role in its pack.
✔ Routinely take toys from the dog's mouth and put them away. Return the toy to the dog when it is least expecting it.
✔ When in a contest with the dog, be sure to win more than half the time. This applies to tug-o-war and other such competitive play.
✔ Always feed the dog after the humans of the household have eaten. Make your superiority evident in every case.

Praise: Honor your dog with your kind words and soft voice for correct performance; ignore mistakes, but persist in training until the task is mastered.
✔ Food treats should be reserved for tasks that are difficult to understand. Give treat rewards on an intermittent basis, not every time you praise the dog for successes.
✔ Rewards take many forms: petting, soft voice tones, play, scratching, or rubbing the dog's ears.
✔ Scolding or nagging are forms of punishment that usually don't get the result you want. Aggressive punishment in the form of physical reprimands will rarely be rewarded by obedience.

When challenged by your dog, begin dominance training all over again.
✔ *"No"* is a command you must teach your dog. It should be reserved for those times when it is misbehaving, not to correct inappropriate obedience responses. Never give a command that you aren't able to teach or enforce immediately.

Note: Be sure not to reward your dog for *nearly correct* performances.

Checklist
Training for Sports

1. **Take the puppy with you to a practice field and get it familiar with tunnels, A-frames, and dog walks, but don't begin jumping.**
2. **Allow the puppy contact with other puppies that are also in training for dog sports. Start your dog's obedience training early in life.**
3. **Begin simple training at or before six months old.**
4. **Before serious training begins, have your Dalmatian examined by a veterinarian for skeletal and circulatory disorders.**
5. **Healthy dogs should be ready at one year of age for intensive training and participating in sports.**
6. **The dog's nutrition while in training or working should be analyzed according to the work. Ask your veterinarian about your dog's diet.**

Activities to Enjoy with Your Dal

As stated before, Dalmatians are active, energetic dogs. Bored Dals that are given too little to do will start showing nuisance behaviors. Apathetic dogs will become moody or try to dig out of your yard; indifferent dogs will jump fences and run away. Dalmatians, being intelligent dogs, thrive on exercise and training. Begin training early, and continue to pursue the sports the dog has learned. Challenge your dog's abilities and provide plenty of tasks for it to learn and master. If your Dalmatian shows interest in Obedience, practice and enter trials. If it's more interested in Agility competition, set up a course and get to work. If Frisbee is the dog's favorite game, teach your Dal to catch and retrieve the plastic disks.

Canine Good Citizen Test

Every Dalmatian deserves this training, which includes exercises that are easily taught at home; all-breed clubs usually offer classes as well. A local dog club representative performs an evaluation and a certificate is awarded for completion of the test. For information about a Canine Good Citizen certificate, contact the AKC (see Information, page 62) or a local dog club. Your Good Citizen Dalmatian will be trustworthy, and will be appreciated by you and your neighbors.

Competitive Dog Sports

Dog sports help keep dogs and their owners in sound physical condition. You will both gain confidence, knowledge, and expertise while you compete with other owners and their dogs. Successful competition will increase your dog's concentration on you, and pinpoint its focus on you and your commands. Focus is fundamental to all successful training. Dog sport competition also teaches the dog to tolerate strange dogs, and performing before a loud, often boisterous audience is excellent experience for you and your dog.

Obedience

Obedience trials are team efforts between dog and handler. Classes of competition are structured to include novices as well as experts. Beginner dogs can start any time after six months of age, and can compete in trials for years. Trials include simple exercises such as *sit* and *down*, and more challenging activities such as scent determination and hurdles that are taken by hand signal off lead.

Tracking

This training is offered by dog clubs and working dog associations (see Information, page 62). Tracking dogs are taught to follow human scents under varying conditions on various terrains. They work in a tracking harness with a long lead, and locate people and scented articles along the track.

Agility

This is a spectator sport that is gaining worldwide popularity. It involves running a course that consists of various standardized obstacles such as tunnels, tires, seesaws, jumps, and weave poles. Dogs compete off lead, and the contest is a timed event. Each mistake or refusal adds seconds to the dog's time. Owners run the course beside their dogs without touching either the dog or the obstacles, motioning toward each obstacle, and giving the dogs verbal encouragement. The course uses the same standard obstacles each time, but their position is varied for each competition. Agility contests provide excellent training for Dalmatians, and teach owner and dog concentration, focus, and trust. An Agility dog must be well bonded to its owner, an obedient and beautifully trained and conditioned athlete.

Search and Rescue

Dalmatians are sometimes trained for rescue work. This highly specialized endeavor requires intense training, practice, and regular work. The proper equipment is not inexpensive. Rescue dogs search wreckage or avalanches for trapped people. They are routinely used to locate persons buried by earthquakes, explosions, and other disasters. Searching in both open ground and dense cover, they are trained to scent out humans, and sometimes to differentiate between the living and the dead.

Fun Matches

If you are interested in showing your Dal but aren't sure about how to get started, fun matches are a good way to learn. A fun match is an informal dog event that is held by a local dog organization. You can get ready for AKC-sanctioned Conformation shows by first competing at fun matches, which often include Obedience, Agility, Tracking, tattoo clinics, and demonstrations of search and rescue, police work, Frisbee, and guide dog activities.

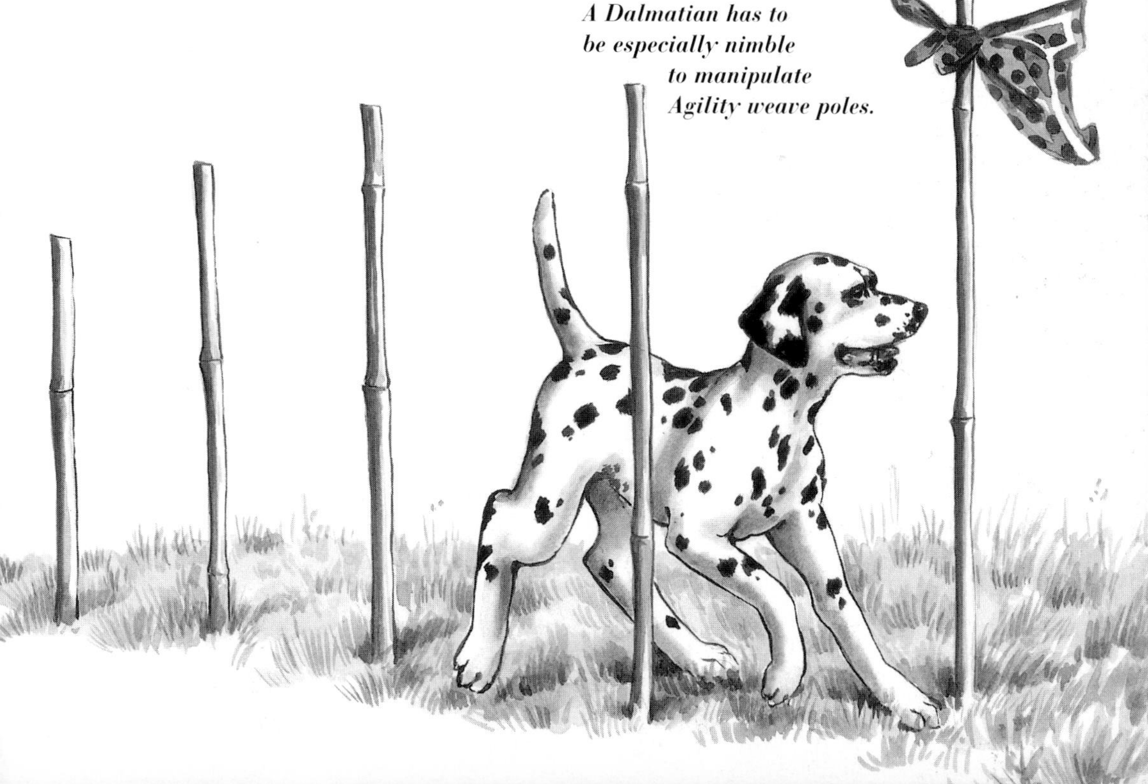

A Dalmatian has to be especially nimble to manipulate Agility weave poles.

CARE IN HEALTH AND SICKNESS

Any dog can become ill or injured, so be prepared. Maintaining your companion's mental and physical health should be a primary goal. This means you should regularly groom your pet, reassess its nutrition, and be alert to changes in its physical condition.

Preventive Care

A few canine infectious diseases and parasites are communicable to humans and other animals. Preventive medicine is logical and essential in order for you to maintain your Dalmatian's good health. It is equally important to recognize the signs and symptoms of illness and know when to consult a veterinarian. Often the best preventive medicine is recognition of early signs, thus avoiding a serious illness.

Regular Vaccinations

Vaccinations given to puppies and throughout life will protect your Dalmatian from fatal and debilitating diseases. Immunizations are usually given at weaning age and must be continued for the rest of the dog's life. Preventable diseases include distemper, hepatitis, leptospirosis, parainfluenza, parvo and corona viruses, Lyme disease, rabies, and several bacterial respiratory diseases. Consult with your veterinarian for appropriate timing of proper vaccinations.

This Dalmatian is good friends with the pony. The breed has an affinity for horses.

For maintenance and protection, your Dalmatian should receive annual boosters, and should always be healthy when the vaccine is administered. Keep an accurate vaccination record for your dog. This is especially necessary when traveling across national borders, and when entering your dog in dog shows, trials, or other competitive events (see page 30).

Regular Worming

Administration of worm medication is necessary *only* when the dog is known to be infested with intestinal parasites. Before worm treatment is given, a stool sample should be taken to your veterinarian for identification of the type of worm to be treated. While a few intestinal parasites are communicable to humans, those instances are rare. Worm treatments should be prescribed or administered by veterinarians, and repeat medication should be given according to the veterinarian's recommendation. Be sure to ask your veterinarian about heartworm prevention.

Worm medication is a poison and should be handled accordingly, whether treating puppies or adult dogs. Different species of worms require different medications. Sometimes infested dogs harbor several different types of intestinal parasites and each is treated independently with a carefully thought-out plan. There is no universal worm medication that is safe and effective for all intestinal parasites. Flea control is essential if you are dealing with tapeworms.

Skin Disorders

Changes in coat: White skins often lead to problems. If your Dalmatian has brownish patches on its coat, accompanied by redness of skin, loss of hair, scabs, and itching, it's time for a trip to your veterinarian. Causes might be nutritional, fungal, parasitic, or allergic. Mange mites are one of the common skin parasites, ringworm is a fungal infection, and food allergies and flea-bite allergies also can cause skin disease. Don't depend on a general skin or coat medication to help!

Note: Hives are skin swellings, accompanied by intense itching and swelling of the eyes or muzzle. These may be the result of a food allergy or bee or other insect stings. Call your veterinarian immediately if these symptoms appear and take your Dal for diagnosis and treatment without delay.

Parasites: Skin parasites are sometimes visible, sometimes not so easy to discover. Any time your dog begins to itch, a magnifying glass will help you to identify the cause.

✔ Ticks are common in some parts of the country. They can be seen with the naked eye and should be removed by gradual pulling with tweezers or gloved fingers. Destroy the tick by putting it into a jar of alcohol. Don't crush it or burn it, and don't handle it with bare fingers!

Note: If the head remains in the skin, it's not serious; simply clean the lesion daily with alcohol.

✔ Fleas and lice are easily seen with the magnifying glass.

✔ Mange mites are microscopic and require a skin scraping to identify.

Note: A veterinarian's help is required to diagnose and treat skin diseases.

Bladder Stones

All Dalmatians have a genetic metabolic deficiency, and are subject to urinary bladder stones. Symptoms include bloody urine, difficulty urinating, and inability to pass urine. Treatment may include medication or surgery. In either case, special diet is indicated to prevent recurrence.

Digestive Organs

Stomach: There may be vomiting, with or without diarrhea, sometimes with blood in stool or vomit, occasionally accompanied by fever and loss of condition. The cause may be an infection, food or chemical poisoning, garbage eating, or systemic disease. Call your veterinarian and schedule an examination.

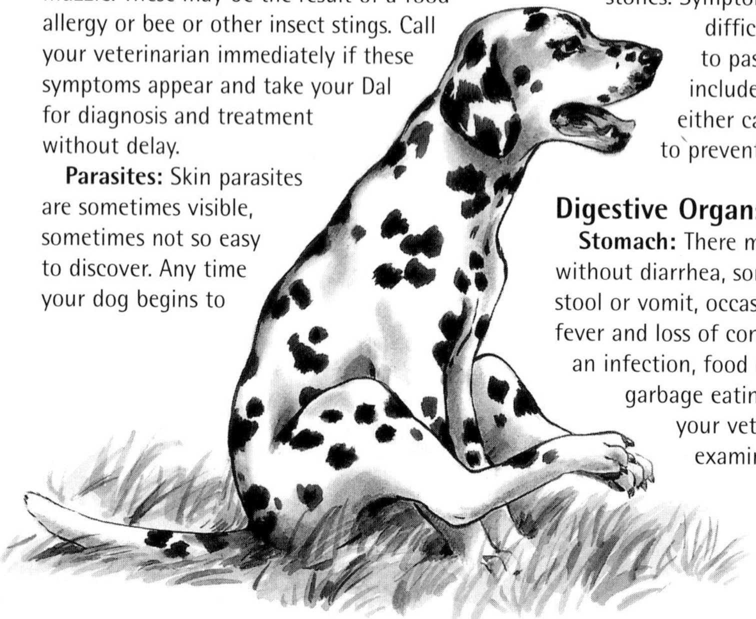

"Scooting" usually indicates anal sac impaction.

Recognizing Disorders and Illnesses

Signs	Causes
Elevated temperature	Various illnesses and systemic infections.
Coughing and gagging, excessive salivation, kennel cough, vomiting, apathy, cramps, or dizziness	Foreign object in mouth or throat, tonsillitis, rabies, pharyngitis, mouth injuries, poisoning, pneumonia, bronchitis, acute gastritis, gastric torsion. Get the dog to the veterinarian quickly!
Vomiting combined with constipation and loss of appetite	Possible intestinal blockage. Check rear for fecal mats; take temperature before visiting the veterinarian.
Dragging rear end ("scooting")	Plugged anal sacs. Take to the veterinarian for relief.
Bad breath	Dental or gum infections, gastritis, eating garbage.
Scratching and shaking head	Ear infection, ear mites, hematoma of ear pinna.
Skin changes	Parasites, allergies, nutritional problems, fungus.
Vomiting attempts, salivation, apathy, and bloated abdomen	Gastric torsion and bloat. Contact your veterinarian for this emergency.
Diarrhea with blood	Enteritis. Call your veterinarian immediately.
Excessive flatulence	Spoiled food, dietary imbalance, garbage eating.
Swollen eyelids and excessive tearing	Conjunctivitis, eyelid foreign body, corneal ulcer, eye injury, allergy, or cherry eye (displaced tear gland appearing as cherry-like growth in inner corner of eye). See your veterinarian immediately.
Limping or trouble moving	Sprains, fractures, infections, hereditary diseases, pad injuries, arthritis, torn ligaments, tendon injuries. Call the veterinarian.

Intestine: If the dog has loose stools or diarrhea without blood or vomiting, the condition is not serious. Fast the dog for 24 hours, then feed cooked rice and cottage cheese mixed with a small amount of cooked, drained hamburger. If no improvement is seen within a day or two, contact the veterinarian.

Lower G.I tract: Constipation is a serious condition and calls for a visit to your veterinarian unless caused by a fecal mat. Check the dog's rear before calling your veterinarian.

Gastric Torsion and Bloat

Excessive salivation, repeated vomiting attempts, distended belly, panting, shock, and apathy are the signs of this usually *fatal* disorder. This syndrome usually follows a big meal, often with exercise immediately after the meal. Surgery must be performed immediately; don't delay seeing your veterinarian!

Prevention: Feed the dog small meals several times daily. Curb all activity for an hour following meals. Put the dog's dish on a platform such as a step, and curtail water after meals.

Special collar keeps the dog from chewing the bandage.

Sense Organs

Ears: When you take your puppy or adopted adult to the veterinarian for its first visit, be sure it is tested for deafness, a genetic defect that sometimes appears in this breed.

The Dalmatian's drop or down ears are susceptible to otitis (see page 36). Ear mites and foreign bodies such as grass awns are often the cause of otitis externa. Tipping the head, shaking, or scratching at the ears are the usual signs of ear canal infections. Wipe the outer ear canals clean with a cotton ball and alcohol, and if there is excessive wax or tenderness, see your veterinarian.

Eyes: Clouding of the cornea indicates a corneal ulcer or infection. Squinting, redness of the conjunctiva, a swollen and protruding third eyelid, or a purulent discharge from the eyes are other signs of problems that should be examined and treated by a veterinarian.

Nose: Bloody or purulent nasal discharges are indications of infections or foreign bodies trapped in the nasal sinuses. These signs should be investigated by a veterinarian.

Movement

Lameness, stilted gait, lack of desire to move around, difficulty getting up, and apparent pain when rising or moving may indicate a serious problem. Take its temperature and examine your Dal. Extend each leg, look at all footpads, check for wounds between toes, and flex all leg joints. If no injury or pain is noted, rest the dog for a day or two. If activity isn't improved after a day of rest, make an appointment with your veterinarian for examination.

Canine Hip Dysplasia (CHD)

Hip dysplasia is a genetic disease that involves the femoral head and the hip socket. In cases of CHD, these structures are hereditar-

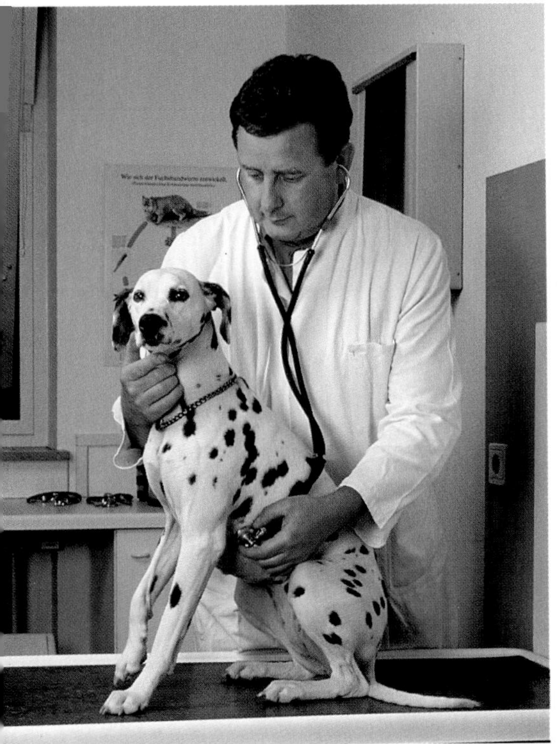

Regular visits to a veterinarian are prerequisites for good health.

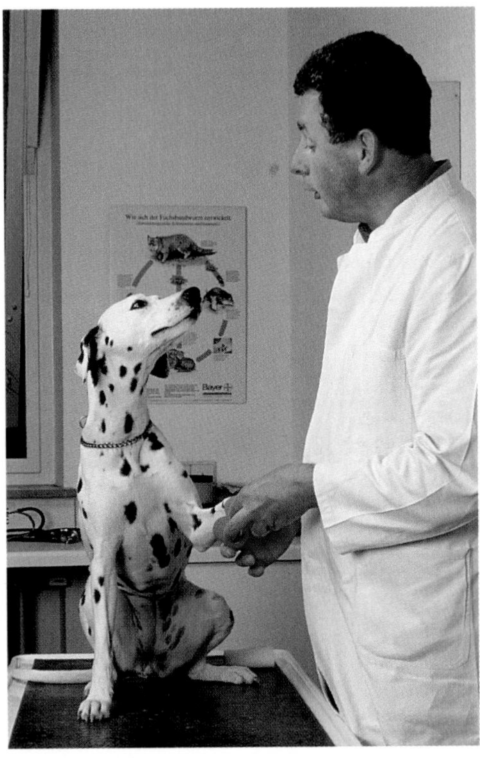

A sympathetic veterinarian has a calming effect on your Dal.

ily malformed, causing osteoarthritis to develop. Signs of CHD may occur early, or as late as six or eight years. Dalmatians are *not* often affected with this disabling disease, but as a precaution, have your dog's hips x-rayed at two years. CHD is not diagnosable by means other than X rays. The condition is not treatable, but if affected, the dog can be given pain relief with medications, or it may be a candidate for hip replacement surgery.

Note: Dalmatians with CHD should not be bred under any circumstances.

OFA

The Orthopedic Foundation for Animals is an organization that reads and classifies pelvic X rays and renders certification of CHD-free dogs. The University of Pennsylvania's veterinary college performs similar x-ray evaluations, and examines dogs for signs of CHD.

Senile Health Problems

Deafness resulting from senile changes is common. Always approach your old dog

TIP

Your Elderly Dalmatian

Aged Dalmatians have specific needs. Often, their joints become weak and painful, and medication is needed for comfort. They sometimes have circulation problems, tumors are common, and eyesight and hearing become weaker or fail.

Unspayed females are subject to mammary tumors, uterine infection, and other diseases.

Unneutered males sometimes suffer from prostatic cancer. Older dogs should be seen by the veterinarian regularly for blood tests and physical examinations. Your old Dal will benefit from periodic examinations that might reveal obscure problems needing attention.

Senior diets should to be adjusted to the animal's age and ability to digest various elements. Often, your veterinarian will prescribe supplements or special dog foods formulated for your elderly Dal.

Exercise should be continued but reduced to shorter treks that are repeated as often as the dog desires. Take care not to tire your elderly dog.

Be particularly careful of exercise during hot weather or on excessively cold days. Give your aging Dal a warm, soft place to sleep.

carefully, preferably from the front. Stamp your feet so it can perceive the vibrations.

Blindness, usually associated with cataracts, is another aging disease. Touching your old dog gently on the head or back will alert it to your presence. Don't confuse the blind dog by rearranging the furniture. If you should change homes when you have a blind dog, lead the dog around the house and yard several times, allowing it to accommodate to its new surroundings while in your company. Old dogs have earned the right to a comfortable retirement; try to minimize the stresses introduced.

Spaying and Neutering

Female dogs: Spaying, or *ovariohysterectomy,* is the best insurance policy you can give your female Dalmatian. It will eliminate her heats, thus controlling reproduction; false pregnancies never occur, nor do mammary tumors, uterine infections, and other cervical and uterine disorders. She will be happier, will concentrate better on training, and will have fewer mood swings. The time for spaying a female is before she comes into her first heat, at about five to six months of age. Cost is minimal in young dogs, and surgical risks are fewer. Spayed females can't compete in AKC Conformation shows, but can participate in Obedience, Agility, and other events.

Male dogs: Castration or *neutering* is recommended before the age of puberty or when your Dal begins to show an interest in females. This surgical procedure relieves the male's reproductive desires, calms an aggressive dog, and increases his attention to training. Neutered males generally make better pets and are easier to train with other dogs. They, like spayed females, may enter Agility competition as well as Obedience trials, but aren't eligible for Conformation shows. Neutering is particularly indicated in cases of aggressive Dalmatians.

Wounds

Injuries should be evaluated immediately. Hemorrhage should be controlled by a pressure bandage, and serious skin tears or deep punctures need a veterinarian's attention. If your dog is hurt badly and resists touching, apply a muzzle before examining its wounds. To prevent further hemorrhage, don't remove a stick from a deep puncture wound. Carry the dog to your car on a blanket or coat and get it to the veterinarian as quickly as possible.

Normal Body Temperature and Medicine Administration

Temperature is easily determined with a digital or glass thermometer. Steady the dog with one hand and insert the lubricated thermometer about 1½ inches (3 cm) into the dog's rectum with the other hand.

Note: Temperatures above 102°F (38.5°C) indicate a fever.

Pills: The easiest way to give a pill is to cover the pill with peanut butter, cream cheese, or any sticky substance your dog will eat. If it isn't interested in eating, gently grasp its muzzle in one hand, squeezing your fingers between its teeth. As its mouth opens, place the pill as far back on the tongue as possible, hold the mouth closed, and stroke its throat or smear some butter on the tip of its nose. It will lick the nose, and in the process will swallow the pill.

Liquids are easier to give. Insert two fingers inside the back corner of your dog's lips and pull outward to form a funnel. Elevate its nose, hold the mouth shut, and pour the liquid medicine into the funnel. It's always easier to take your Dal's temperature, or give a pill or liquid medicine if you have another person to help.

A sick Dalmatian needs rest and attention.

INDEX

"Will you be my friend?" This Dal puppy has a toy companion.

Addresses

American Kennel Club
260 Madison Avenue
New York, NY 10016

Canadian Kennel Club
180–89 Skyway Avenue
Etobicoke, Ontario M9W 6R4
Canada
416-675-5511

Dalmatian Club of America, Inc.
Mrs. Sharon Boyd, Secretary
2316 McCrary Road
Richmond, TX 77469-9696

Orthopedic Foundation for Animals, Inc.
Hip Registry
2300 East Nifong Boulevard
Columbia, MO 65201-3856

United Kennel Club
100 East Kilgore Road
Kalamazoo, MI 49002-5584

Lost Dog Recovery
AKC Animal Companion Recovery
5580 Centerview Drive Suite 250
Raleigh, NC 27606-3394
1-800-252-7894

Microchip Pet Identification System
For a complimentary HomeAgain information kit, call 1-800-2Find-Pet; visit the web site at http://www.spanimalhealth.com/ha.htm.

Pet Sitters International
418 East King Street
King, NC 27021-9163
336-983-9222
http://www.petsitin@ols.net

Helpful Books

Alderton, David. *The Dog Care Manual.* Hauppauge, New York: Barron's Educational Series, Inc., 1984.

Baer, Ted. *Communicating with Your Dog.* Hauppauge, New York: Barron's Educational Series, Inc., 1989.

Frye, Frederic I. *First Aid for Your Dog.* Hauppauge, New York: Barron's Educational Series, Inc., 1987.

Klever, Ulrigh. *The Complete Book of Dog Care.* Hauppauge, New York: Barron's Educational Series, Inc., 1989.

Vine, Louis L., D.V.M. *Your Dog, His Health and Happiness.* New York: Prentice Hall, 1986.

Whitney, Leon, D.V.M. and Whitney, George, D.V.M. *The Complete Book of Dog Care.* New York: Doubleday, 1984.

Woodhouse, Barbara. *No Bad Dogs.* New York: Summit Books, 1982.

Useful Magazines

AKC Gazette
260 Madison Avenue
New York, NY 10016

Dog Fancy
P.O. Box 53264
Boulder, CO 80322-3264

Dog World
PJS Publications, Inc.
2 News Plaza, P.O. Box 1790
Peoria, IL 61656

The Author

Katharina Schlegl-Kofler has been involved for many years in dog training. She has conducted puppy play days and training courses for all breeds of dogs.

The Photographer

Monika Wegler is a professional photographer and author of animal books. Animal portraits are a significant part of her photography work, as are behavioral and motion studies of dogs and cats.

The Illustrator

Renate Holzner works as a freelance illustrator. Her broad field of expertise ranges from line drawings to photorealistic illustrations and computer graphics.

The Translator

Eric Bye, M.A., is an accredited freelance translator who works in German, French, Spanish, and English at his office in Vermont. He is also a life-long dog owner.

The Consulting Editor

Dan Rice, D.V.M., is author of several Barron's books, including *Brittanys, Chesapeake Bay Retrievers,* and *The Well-mannered Cat.*

Important Note

The guidelines in this book for the maintenance of Dalmatians refer primarily to normally developed animals of flawless breeding, and consequently to healthy, essentially impeccable dogs. Anyone who takes in a grown dog must be aware that it has already been influenced by its experiences with people.

Even well-trained dogs may cause damage to someone else's property, or even cause accidents. It is therefore always advisable to take out liability insurance that covers your dog. Also make sure your dog gets all the necessary protective inoculations and is wormed; otherwise, there are increased health risks to dog and humans.

Any time your Dalmatian shows signs of illness (see page 55), you should consult a veterinarian. Consult your own doctor if you are bitten by your dog. Some people are allergic to animal hair. If you are not sure, consult your doctor before you buy a dog.

Photos

Page 1: This puppy has been digging in the sandbox.
Pages 2–3: Two Dalmatian puppies, five weeks old, sniff a Dalmatian-Rex rabbit.
Pages 4–5: Two Dalmatians jump over an Agility hurdle.
Pages 6–7: Three Dalmatian puppies, seven weeks old, in their own bed.
Pages 64–65: Mother Dalmatian with her pups.

Original title of the book in German is *Dalmatiner*
Translation from the German by Eric A. Bye
Adapted by Dan Rice, D.V.M.

All inquiries should be addressed to:
Barron's Educational Series, Inc.
250 Wireless Boulevard
Hauppauge, NY 11788
http://www.barronseduc.com

Library of Congress Catalog Card No. 99-21104
International Standard Book No. 0-7641-0941-3

Library of Congress Cataloging-in-Publication Data
Schlegl-Kofler, Katharina.
[Dalmatiner. English]
Dalmations / Katharina Schlegl-Kofler ; photographs, Monika Wegler ; illustrations, Renate Holzner ; [translation from the German by Eric A. Bye].
p. cm. – (A Complete pet owner's manual)
Includes bibliographical references (p.).
ISBN 0-7641-0941-3
1. Dalmatian dog. I. Title. II. Series.
SF429.D3S38613 1999
636.72–dc21 99-21104
CIP

Printed in Hong Kong
9 8 7 6 5 4 3 2 1

EXPERT ADVICE

1 How much does a Dalmatian cost?	*The price for a pet-quality puppy from a reputable breeder may be $500 or more.*
2 What effect does deafness have on a dog's life?	*Entirely deaf Dalmatian puppies should be euthanized. Deafness in one ear does not detract materially from a Dalmatian, although it should be neutered.*
3 What is the difference between black- and brown-spotted Dalmatians?	*There are no differences in bearing, nature, or health; black is dominant, brown is recessive.*
4 What kinds of undesirable markings are found on Dalmatians?	*Large blotches on the body or around the eyes, as well as brown and black spots on the same dog are undesirable. These dogs should not be bred.*
5 How can you tell you're buying a healthy puppy?	*By its shiny, smooth coat, clear eyes, and clean nose; the anal region is clean; the puppy is well nourished and has a little baby fat.*

An expert answers the 10 most frequently asked questions on how to keep Dalmatians.

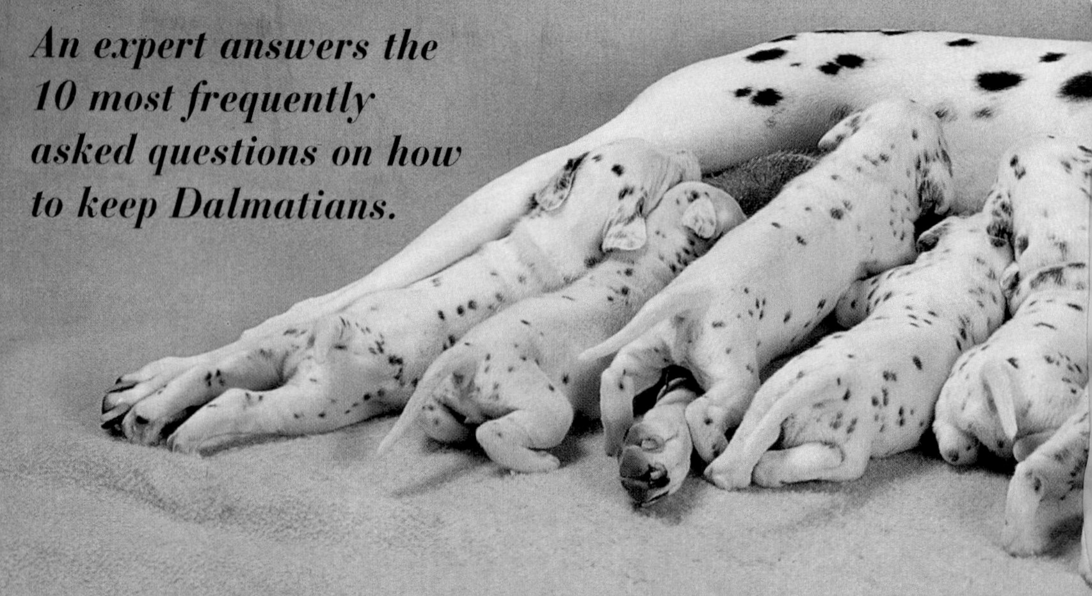